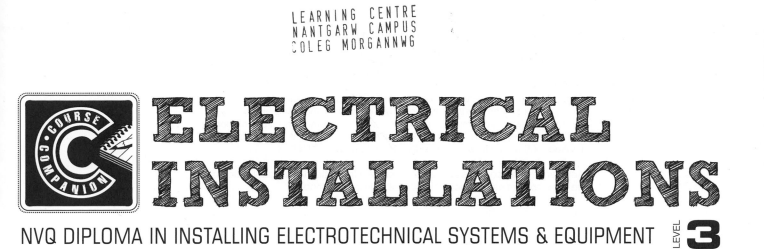

ELECTRICAL INSTALLATIONS

COURSE COMPANION

NVQ DIPLOMA IN INSTALLING ELECTROTECHNICAL SYSTEMS & EQUIPMENT LEVEL 3

John Blaus

Published in 2011 by:
Nelson Thornes Ltd
Delta Place
27 Bath Road
CHELTENHAM
GL53 7TH
United Kingdom

11 12 13 14 15 / 10 9 8 7 6 5 4 3 2 1

A catalogue record for this book is available from the British Library

ISBN 978 1 4085 0876 3

Page make-up by Wearset Ltd

Printed and bound in Spain by GraphyCems

Every effort has been made to contact copyright holders and we apologise if any have been overlooked. Should copyright have been unwittingly infringed in this book, the owners should contact the publishers who will make corrections at reprint.

Acknowledgements
Alamy p10 (Tim Scrivener), p59T1 (David J. Green); **John Blaus** p81, p82, p83, p84; **Fotolia.com** p14 (Elenathewise), p17 (manfredxy), p19 (zentilia), p22 (Sophia Winters), p40 (auremar), p53 (Sandor Kacso), p58B (Willee Cole), p58T (Franz Pfluegl), p59T2 (Oleksandr Dorokhov), p59T3 (John Tomaselli), p59T4 (AlexSander), p59T5 (Serghei Velusceac), p59T6 (Fatbob), p59T7 (Serghei Velusceac), p59T8 (skaljac), p60T1 (Les Cunliffe), p60T2 (ws2000), p60T3 (Paul Bodea), p60T4 (Serghei Velusceac), p78 (Leonid Smirnov), p87 (m.schuckart); **iStock** p1 (Wayne Pillinger), p24 (Dmitry Mordvintsev), p65 (mümin inan), p69 (Andrew Howe)

Contents

Introduction

Welcome to the Level 3 Electrical Installations Course Companion. It is literally a companion to support you throughout your course and record your progress!

This workbook style book is designed to be used alongside **any** student book you are using. It is packed full of activities for you to complete in order to check your knowledge and reinforce the essential skills you need for this qualification.

Features of the Course Companion are:

Unit opener – this page contains a brief introduction to each unit along with the learning objectives you need to achieve

Key knowledge – the underpinning knowledge you must know is summarised throughout each unit

Activities – a wide variety of learning activities are provided to complete in your Companion. Each activity is linked to one of the Personal, Learning and Thinking Skills to help you practice these fundamental skills:

– Reflective Learner

– Creative Thinker

– Teamworker

– Self Manager

– Independent Enquirer

– Effective Participator

You will also notice additional icons that appear on different activities, which link to the following core skills and also to rights and responsibilities in the workplace:

 – Literacy

– Numeracy

– ICT

 – Employment, Rights and Responsibilities

Key terms – during your course you'll come across new words or new terms that you may not have heard before, so definitions for these have been provided

Your questions answered – your expert author, John Blaus, answers some of the burning questions you may have as you work through the units

Quick Quiz – At the end of each unit you will find a multiple choice quiz. Answering these will check that you have fully understood what you have learnt.

Good luck!

UNIT 301
Understanding health and safety legislation, practices and procedures

Health and safety is an essential part of your working life. It could mean the difference between life and death.

Statistics compiled by the Health and Safety Executive show:

➤ Construction has the largest number of fatal injuries of the main industry groups. In 2009–10 there were 42 work-related deaths. This is the third highest rate of fatal injuries, behind agriculture and extractive industries.
➤ Construction accounted for 35 per cent (276 cases) of all reported injuries involving high falls and 24.8 per cent (89) involving electricity.
➤ In 2009–10, 3.3 million working days were lost in construction due to workplace injury and work-related ill health.

(www.hse.gov.uk/statistics/industry/construction/index.htm)

It is the responsibility of both the employer and the employee to reduce the risk of accidents by adhering to health and safety legislation. The employer should provide safe working conditions and ensure all staff are trained in health and safety procedures. The employee has to follow health and safety procedures and to ensure appropriate personal protective equipment is worn on-site.

You will need to understand the following:
➤ how relevant health and safety legislation applies in the workplace
➤ the procedures for dealing with health and safety in the work environment
➤ the procedures for establishing a safe working environment
➤ the requirements for identifying and dealing with hazards in the work environment

Key knowledge

➤ Health and safety legislation and procedures

➤ Risk assessments

➤ Personal protective equipment

➤ Hazards and fire prevention

Health and safety legislation

ACTIVITY

There are 11 main health and safety regulations that affect the construction industry. These regulations are listed below, along with a brief description of each. Your task is to match the appropriate description to each regulation by writing the correct letter in each box.

A Health and Safety at Work Act	• The main rules that cover health and safety in the workplace • Provides safety in the workplace • Protects visitors and the public	
B Provision and Use of Work Equipment regulations	• Rules covering dangerous solids, liquids or gases and how they should be used and stored • Actions you and your employer must take to protect your health and the health of others	
C Personal Protective Equipment at Work regulations	• A legal framework that covers all aspects of electrical work and equipment to be used. Failure to follow these rules could lead to prosecution	
D Control of Substances Hazardous to Health (COSHH regulations)	• Rules covering the use of hard hats, impact goggles, ear defenders, protective gloves, overalls, safety footwear and high-visibility clothing	

E Workplace (Health and Safety at Work regulations)	• Regulations that require employers to:
	   • analyse workstations to assess and reduce risks
	   • ensure workstations meet specified minimum requirements
	   • plan work activities so they include breaks or changes of activity	

F Management of Health and Safety at Work regulations	• A legal requirement to do with your health and safety in the workplace • Your employer must carry out a risk assessment and act upon the findings to minimise risks	
G Manual Handling Operations regulations	• Regulations to ensure that workplaces meet the health, safety and welfare needs of all members of a workforce, including people with disabilities	
H Electricity at Work regulations	• Regulations requiring mandatory training for anyone likely to be exposed to asbestos fibres at work (see Regulation 10). This includes maintenance workers and others who may come into contact with or who may disturb asbestos (for example, cable installers), as well as those involved in asbestos removal work	
I Working at Height regulations	• Regulations that place duties upon employers in respect of their own employees; identical duties are placed on self-employed workers in respect of their own safety • Regulations that seek to reduce the incidence of injury and ill-health arising from manual handling of loads at work. More than one in four of all reportable injuries are caused during manual handling	

J	Control of Asbestos at Work regulations	• A summary of what you need to do to comply with the Working at Height 2005 Regulations. Some industry/trade associations may have produced more detailed guidance about working at height	
K	Display Screen Equipment at Work regulations	• Guidance to protect people's health and safety in relation to equipment they use at work • Equipment that includes electric drilling machines and any piece of equipment provided by you or your employer	

ACTIVITY

In each of the following situations, which of the regulations listed has been broken?

1. An electrician fails to wear a hard hat on-site.

2. Mains-voltage equipment is used on a construction site.

3. Ceiling tiles containing asbestos are disposed of in a skip.

4. A worker uses a ladder with a broken rung while installing security lighting.

Health and safety procedures

In order to comply with health and safety legislation, all construction sites have to comply with standard procedures. Each site has to inform site operatives of the relevant procedures for that site. Visitors and contractors must always have a site induction.

ACTIVITY

On-site health and safety procedures

Outline the procedures you would follow for either your current workplace or your training centre in order to comply with health and safety requirements.

1. How would you summon emergency services to the site?

2. What information would the emergency services require from you?

3. Describe how you would raise the alarm and evacuate the premises.

4. How would you identify the correct escape routes?

5. What would you do if you saw a fire?

6. What would you do if a colleague experienced an electric shock?

Who is responsible for health and safety?

ACTIVITY

In the following table, tick the job title of the person responsible for hazard and accident prevention. In some instances, more than one person may be responsible.

Hazard	Employer	Employees	Customer	Safety officer	HSE inspectors	Trade union representative	Environmental health officer
Working in poor light conditions							
Poor housekeeping of site							
Having a hangover							
Insufficient supervision							
Protective guards are not provided around machinery							
A ladder with broken rungs is being used							
Faulty personal protective equipment is being issued							
A fire exit is blocked							
The wrong safety signs are posted on walls							
There are inadequate toilet facilities and access to drinking water							
The employer is not informed of the dangerous condition of the building							
Mains voltage is used on a new building site							
There is too much overtime working							
The accident book is not kept up to date							
A death occurs on-site due to a breach of the Working at Height regulations							

Establishing a safe working environment

Risk assessments

Risk assessments are an important element of health and safety. They are carried out to identify any potential **risks** to individuals. The intention is to make sure that no-one gets hurt or becomes ill due to work activity. It is a legal requirement for organisations to carry out a risk assessment of the workplace. There are five principles to risk assessments:

1. identify **hazards**

2. decide who might be harmed and how

3. evaluate the risks and decide whether existing precautions are adequate

4. record the findings of the assessment

5. review the assessment and, if necessary, revise it.

ACTIVITY

Performing risk assessments
Complete the risk assessment shown in the table for each of the given scenarios.

Hazard	Who might be harmed?	Existing controls	Future actions
Manual handling: in the stores, movement of equipment and components			
Noise: for contracting electricians working on a factory floor in a food processing plant			
Slips, trips and falls on a new two-storey building site			
Electricians working outdoors at height			
Electricians installing and glueing plastic conduit in confined spaces			

Personal protective equipment

All construction operatives should be issued with the correct **personal protective equipment (PPE)** for the work they do and the situation they operate in. Personnel should also be trained in the correct use of PPE.

PPE can protect the user from injuries caused by chemicals, heat, impact, electrical hazards and infection, for job-related occupational health and safety purposes.

ACTIVITY

Identifying the appropriate PPE
For each of the following situations, outline what PPE should be used and explain why.

1. An electrician working in a domestic residence.

2. An electrician installing outside security lighting on a three-storey building.

3. An electrician drilling holes in masonry at head height.

4. An electrician cutting metal trunking with a hacksaw.

5. An electrician installing cables in a working factory.

6. An electrician installing solar panels on the roof of a house.

ACTIVITY

PPE is an important issue for health and safety. What are the responsibilities of the employer and the employee to ensure PPE is correctly used on-site?

Employer	Employee
•	•
•	•
•	•
•	•

Identifying and dealing with hazards in the work environment

The four main hazards that pose a risk to electricians are:

1 electric shock

2 burns

3 fires

4 explosions.

Ten common hazards an electrician faces in the workplace are:

1 slippery or uneven surfaces

2 trailing leads or cables (trip hazard)

3 temporary electrical supplies (electric shock)

4 presence of dust and fumes (respiratory problems)

5 handling and transporting equipment or materials (back injury, manual handling)

6 fire

7 working at height with insufficient safety equipment

8 faulty equipment

9 incorrect use of power and hand tools

10 working with contaminants and irritants.

ACTIVITY

Working in pairs, identify 10 hazards in the workplace that you can think of. Think about how they can be reduced or avoided. Write down your findings as if you were preparing to give a presentation.

Employers are required to provide safety signs in a variety of situations. There are four different types of safety sign used:

1 prohibition signs

2 warning signs

3 mandatory

4 safe way to go signs.

In addition, there are symbols that are used on the packaging of hazardous substances to comply with the Chemicals (Hazard Information and Packaging for Supply) regulations 2009. These are black pictures on an orange background, though new images are coming into effect.

ACTIVITY

Recognising health and safety symbols

Name the symbol type, give its meaning and an example of a situation in which it may be used.

You can use the internet or other sources in your research.

Symbol		Type	Meaning	Situation
Original	New			
		Warning sign	Explosive	Leaking gas main

ACTIVITY

Outline three workplace situations which could be hazardous. Describe the hazard and suggest how it could be avoided or minimised. For example:

Situation: during a standard rewiring of an old house an apprentice electrician has to drill into a wall.

Hazard: the apprentice may drill into a live cable.

Prevention: the apprentice should check for live cables before drilling.

Situation:

Hazard:

Prevention:

Situation:

Hazard:

Prevention:

Situation:

Hazard:

Prevention:

Fire prevention

Fire could be the worst kind of hazard on a construction site. All fires should be investigated, however small.

Remember, there are three elements that need to be present for a fire to start:

➤ fuel – anything that will burn (for example, wood, paper, flammable liquid)

➤ oxygen or air

➤ heat – a minimum temperature is needed, but a naked flame, match or spark is sufficient to start a fire.

Removing any one of these elements will extinguish or prevent a fire.

REFLECT

ACTIVITY

Fires can be prevented if employees take care of their work environment. List six ways you could reduce the risk of fire on a construction site.

1.

2.

3.

4.

5.

6.

THINK

ACTIVITY

Fire-fighting first actions
Listed below are five steps to take for tackling a fire if you are the first person to discover it.

Number the sentences in the correct sequence for tackling a fire.

...... Evacuate the area.

...... Fight the fire (if you are trained to do so), but avoiding endangering lives.

...... Raise the alarm.

...... Identify the appropriate fire extinguisher to use.

...... Close doors and windows to prevent the fire spreading.

Fire extinguishers

There is more than one type of fire extinguisher. The type of fire extinguisher you should use depends on the nature of the fire. All fire extinguishers are colour-coded, so you can see at a glance which type it is, what it contains and what type of fire it should be used on.

British Standard BS7863 requires that an identifying block of colour must now be placed above the operating instructions, and must cover 3–5 per cent of the extinguisher area. The most common types of fire extinguisher available are shown here.

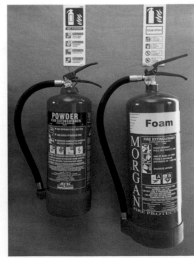

ACTIVITY

Identifying the correct fire extinguisher

Complete the table, indicating what each fire extinguisher contains and the type of fire it should be used on.

Fire extinguisher label colour	Fire extinguisher contains	Type of fire this extinguisher can be used on
White		
Blue		
Cream		
Black		
Green		
Yellow		

ACTIVITY

Find as many different fire extinguishers as you can in your workplace or training centre. If you don't know where to look, then ask your colleagues. Make a list of which fire extinguishers you found, where you found them and the types of fire they will put out. Be prepared to share your findings with the whole class.

Extinguisher	Location	Used on

ACTIVITY

Health and safety crossword

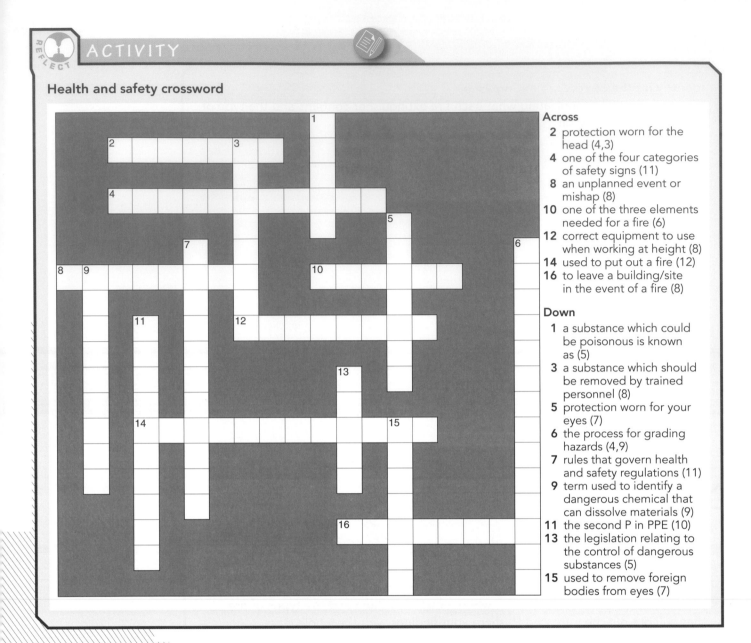

Across

2 protection worn for the head (4,3)

4 one of the four categories of safety signs (11)

8 an unplanned event or mishap (8)

10 one of the three elements needed for a fire (6)

12 correct equipment to use when working at height (8)

14 used to put out a fire (12)

16 to leave a building/site in the event of a fire (8)

Down

1 a substance which could be poisonous is known as (5)

3 a substance which should be removed by trained personnel (8)

5 protection worn for your eyes (7)

6 the process for grading hazards (4,9)

7 rules that govern health and safety regulations (11)

9 term used to identify a dangerous chemical that can dissolve materials (9)

11 the second P in PPE (10)

13 the legislation relating to the control of dangerous substances (5)

15 used to remove foreign bodies from eyes (7)

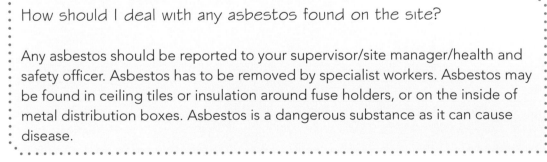

Your questions answered...

How should I deal with any asbestos found on the site?

Any asbestos should be reported to your supervisor/site manager/health and safety officer. Asbestos has to be removed by specialist workers. Asbestos may be found in ceiling tiles or insulation around fuse holders, or on the inside of metal distribution boxes. Asbestos is a dangerous substance as it can cause disease.

QUICK QUIZ
HOW MUCH DO YOU KNOW ABOUT HEALTH AND SAFETY LEGISLATION, PRACTICES AND PROCEDURES?

1. Name four components in a first-aid box.

2. Where should the accident report book be kept on a building site?

3. What would you do if a colleague cut their hand on a metal conduit?

4. What symbol is used to indicate the location of the first-aid box/station?

5. Give examples of where asbestos may be encountered on a building site.

6. What procedure would you follow if you discovered asbestos in ceiling tiles when rewiring an old building?

7. Define what is meant by the term 'hazard' in relation to health and safety legislation.

8. What does CHIP stand for and what are its implications for electricians?

9. What are the four main hazards that pose a risk to electricians?

UNIT 302

Understanding environmental legislation, working practices and the principles of environmental technology systems

As part of the global trend towards minimising the risk to our natural environment, all countries have set out policies directing organisations to help us achieve a 'greener' society. The UK government has set the target of reducing all greenhouse gas emissions by 80 per cent by 2050.

The Carbon Reduction Commitment Energy Efficiency Scheme is part of the government's drive to get large employers to reduce their carbon footprint by using energy-efficient processes. In addition, the government has set out policies affecting all industrial sectors, regarding the effective disposal of waste materials.

Construction businesses can have a number of impacts on the environment:

➤ air emissions, such as dust from earth works or emissions from plant and equipment
➤ land contamination, which can occur when developing historically contaminated sites
➤ noise pollution from operation of plant and equipment
➤ waste disposal, such as spoil, off-cuts and other building materials
➤ water discharges, such as removing water from construction sites.

In this unit you will review the main legislation affecting the electrical and construction industries.

You will need to understand the following:
➤ the environmental legislation, working practices and principles relevant to work activities
➤ how work methods and procedures can reduce material wastage and impact on the environment
➤ how and where environmental technology systems can be applied

Key knowledge

➤ Current legislation

➤ Environmental technology systems

➤ Waste reduction

➤ Reducing waste

LEARNING CENTRE
NANTGARW CAMPUS
COLEG MORGANNWG

Current legislation

Environmental legislation is continually updated as new technologies become available to support the green environment. The NetRegs website lists all current legislation for each of the regions within the UK (www.netregs.gov.uk/netregs/legislation/current/110552.aspx). Another website that can be used to search for any UK-based legislation is www.legislation.gov.uk.

Code for Sustainable Homes

ACTIVITY

On 13 December 2006, the Department for Communities and Local Government (CLG) launched the Code for Sustainable Homes, a new national standard for sustainable design and construction of new homes. The Code goes further than current Building Regulations but is entirely voluntary, and is intended to help promote even higher standards of sustainable design.

As part of its drive to reduce carbon emissions, the government wants to reduce the United Kingdom's carbon emissions from housing by one-third by 2050.

By 2015 no old home will lack basic energy-efficiency measures. From 2016 all new homes will be built to a new **zero-carbon** standard. By 2020 seven million homes will have been upgraded to significantly improve their energy performance. By 2050 virtually the nation's entire housing stock will have reached the zero-carbon standard.

This will require a complete transformation of the housing stock over the coming decades. For the house-building industry, that's a lot of work – and a big opportunity.

The Code for Sustainable Homes measures the whole home as a complete package, assessing its sustainability against nine categories. Use the internet to find out what those categories are.

1.

2.

3.

4.

5.

6.

7.

8.

9.

ACTIVITY

Carry out some internet-based research to find out about the following environmental legislation. You need to find out the year the legislation was set and identify three key impacts the legislation has on the electrical or construction trades.

Title	Year	Summary of content
Environmental Protection Act		1 2 3
Hazardous Waste Regulations		1 2 3
Pollution Prevention and Control Act		1 2 3
Control of Pollution Act		1 2 3
Control of Noise at Work Regulations		1 2 3
Packaging (Essential Requirements) Regulations		1 2 3
Environment Act		1 2 3
Waste Electrical and Electronic Equipment Regulations		1 2 3

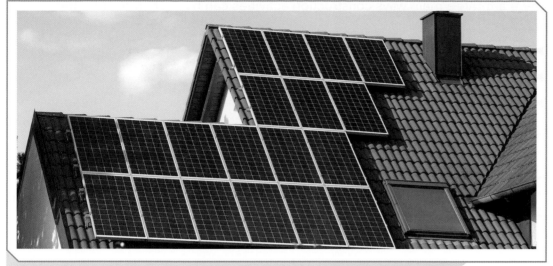

Figure 2.1: Solar panels on new buildings can help reduce carbon emissions.

key terms

Zero carbon a standard in energy production and use that treats homes as individual energy 'islands' which must generate all the power and heat they need. Current recommendations are that the 'built performance' emissions from new homes should not exceed:

- $10\,kg\,CO_2(eq)/m^2/$ year for detached houses
- $11\,kg\,CO_2(eq)/m^2/$ year for other houses
- $14\,kg\,CO_2(eq)/m^2/$ year for low-rise apartment blocks.

ACTIVITY

Use www.communities.gov.uk (Code for Sustainable Homes, Building Regs Part P) to find three main issues for electrical installations (lighting and electrical safety in the home) outlined in the Building Regulations and the Code for Sustainable Homes.

1.

2.

3.

Protecting the environment

ACTIVITY

Define in your own words the terms natural environment and built environment.

Natural environment:

Built environment:

There are three main ways construction activities can have an impact on the natural environment. These are:

➤ land contamination

➤ air pollution

➤ pollution of water courses.

ACTIVITY

For each of the following scenarios, identify what impact the work activities may have on the environment. What actions could you take to reduce any negative impact? You can use books and/or the internet to research this.

Scenario	Land	Air	Water	Measures to take
You are part of a construction company with the contract to develop a former psychiatric hospital into a residential development. There are substantial grounds as part of the hospital property. You are developing a number of apartments and houses on the site. Consider: the presence of asbestos; drug disposal areas; the former incinerator; the presence of chemicals; landscaping.				
The local planning department has finally given approval for the construction of six wind-powered turbines in an area of natural beauty. Local residents have offered strong opposition to the project. Your every move is being monitored by environmentalists. Consider: access to the site; disposal of waste materials; noise and disturbance to residents.				
A disused industrial unit is to be cleared for the development of a new distribution centre for a major retailer. The old building contains hundreds of fluorescent and sodium lights, miles of old lead sheath cabling and some oil-filled transformers. You are tasked with overseeing the removal of the obsolete products. Consider: correct waste disposal; correct PPE; change of use for the site.				

Scenario	Land	Air	Water	Measures to take
The local college has recently been granted permission for a new build at a waterfront location. The site was a former gas works. Consider: reclaiming the land; traffic issues; energy efficiency of the building.				
The M6 motorway is being expanded from a three-lane to a four-lane motorway between major urban areas and the picturesque lake district. Consider: the impact on urban and natural environments; water, air and land pollution.				
Heathrow has received government permission to develop its additional runway. You are one of the contractors working on the expansion programme. Consider: the area to be developed; access to the site; increased traffic.				

Figure 2.2: Wind turbines are an alternative method of producing electricity, but their appearance, noise and operation worries some environmental groups.

Reducing waste

The more waste we generate, the more we have to dispose of. Some methods of waste disposal release **air pollutants** and **greenhouse gases** into the atmosphere. Waste **recycling** offers one means of reducing the impacts of waste disposal on the atmosphere, but there are other methods of waste reduction that are more environmentally friendly.

key terms

Air pollutants chemicals, particulate matter or biological materials released into the atmosphere that cause harm or discomfort to humans or other living organisms, or which damage the natural environment.
Greenhouse gases gases in the atmosphere that trap the sun's energy and thereby contribute to rising surface temperatures. The main greenhouse gas that contributes to climate change is carbon dioxide (CO_2), a byproduct of burning fossil fuels.
Recycling passing a substance through a system that enables that substance to be reused. Waste recycling involves the collection, separation and clean-up of waste materials. Recycling waste means that fewer new products and consumables need to be produced, saving raw materials and reducing energy consumption.

ACTIVITY

In the table, identify which items of waste material are hazardous to health and which can be recycled. State the most appropriate way of disposing of each item.

Item	Hazardous (Y/N)	Recyclable (Y/N)	Safe method of disposing of this item
Zinc chloride battery			
Paper-based employee records			
Old glazed units (timber frame)			
Asbestos			
Electric cables (copper)			
Electric cables (aluminium)			
Wooden floorboards			
Fluorescent tubes			
Tungsten halogen lamp			
Fuses			
PVC trunking			
Plasma television			
Cathode ray tubes			

ACTIVITY

The disposal of waste costs the construction industry more and more each year. Effective waste management can help construction companies increase profits, become more resource efficient, minimise waste and disposal costs and comply with new regulations. Construction companies need to start identifying ways to reduce the amount of waste disposed of during the construction process.

Think of ways you can reduce, reuse or recycle materials used in electrical installation practices. Listed below are a number of statements. Tick whether you think each of this is a *Do* or a *Do not* for good practice in waste management.

	Do ☑	Do not ☒
Train staff about the Site Waste Management Planning Regulations 2008.		
Allow your waste to be removed by an unlicensed waste carrier.		
Take waste seriously and identify the true cost of waste and the real value of resource efficiency.		
Leave materials that are easily damaged out in the rain or in a muddy area.		
Educate yourself and your staff to think about how they can reduce waste and increase profit through resource efficiency.		
Mix hazardous waste with non-hazardous or inert waste.		
Incorporate the requirements of your site waste management plan into the site induction.		
Arrange for waste materials to be sorted into categories for recycling.		
Over-order materials that you don't need.		

ACTIVITY

ACTIVITY

Who would be held liable if you incorrectly disposed of fluorescent light tubes on a building site?

Environmental technology systems

Green technology or clean technology is the application of environmental science to conserve the natural environment and resources, and to curb the negative impacts of human involvement. **Sustainable development** is the core of environmental technologies.

ACTIVITY

Complete the table, identifying the uses for the various sustainable development technologies and any limitations. Use books and/or the internet to research your answers.

Environmental technology system	Application – where should this be used?	Limitations of usage
Solar energy (photovoltaic cells)		
Wind energy generation (micro and macro)		
Heat pumps		
Combined heat and power (CHP), including micro CHP		
Grey water recycling		
Rainwater harvesting		
Biomass heating		
Solar thermal hot water heating		

Figure 2.3: Rainwater harvesting is just one of many sustainable development technologies that are becoming more widely available.

ACTIVITY

Find the words in the word search and put a circle around each.

```
R P E D U T C O P P E R C A B L E C E Y O U R E
C H A R B N O I T A N I M A T N O C D N A L O B
N O F O O E G N T P R I N H T Y H R N K M J Y U
N T S C W M R Q O Q Y N B C E K G H K K J D F T
C O L L V N E T N I Y R E T T A B R F Q V B T T
E V A Q N O Y W R J T L L B J G T T E Z H M N N
L O I V T R W V K T M U Z F Z Z W P G N C T R E
T L R C T I A M M F V M L W Q N M L U T E P K C
T T E R V V T B Y Q S C T L Q T T M L M A Z J S
O A T Z Y N E Q D U R M K K O N E X N C P L D E
B I A L Y E R Y S N B M Z M F P X S K W Y S R R
C C M Z W A S T E D I S P O S A L A I E F E Q O
I R W T Z W A H T T H V F H L T G X L O W T N U
T Q A G N I T A E H S S A M O I B B Q O N X N L
S C R I N N J L T R U H T T N W A T P E G O E F
A N R A N N J B R E O W Q G R C Z R I Q I M M G
L H B E F W L M N U D X R B D N A C M T I T F F
P L L G C T A L W S R Y B A R L I J A S Z K H K
E J N M M Y M T P E A Q E M O F L L S P Z K X Q
L C G N N C C P E L Z L K S F T S I F P L D C T
M L B T N H J L T R A C H E K I O T D B R W R C
Z T K L Z T K Y E T H M T N G N B N L G W T R X
X L T R G F W M Z R N L C E S L W Z V P B K L C
M W I N D P O W E R X K L M H T M R X F R P R H
```

battery
biomass heating
copper cable
efficient
emissions
energy
environment
fluorescent tube
grey water
hazardous
heat pumps
land contamination
lead cable
legislation
noise
packaging
photovoltaic
plastic bottle
pollution
rainwater
raw materials
recycle
reuse
solar power
sustainable
waste disposal
wind power

Your questions answered...

I often hear people talking about grey water recycling. What is this?

Grey water gets its name from its cloudy appearance and from its status as being between fresh drinking water (known as 'white water') and sewage water ('black water'). In a household context, grey water is the leftover water from baths, showers, hand basins and washing machines only.

Water from contaminating sources such as toilets is considered black water.

Grey water can be recycled on-site for uses such as landscape irrigation and constructed wetlands.

QUICK QUIZ

1. Which regulation covers the disposal of old computers?

2. You see a worker on your site throw waste cement into the local stream. Who should you report this to?

3. Waste water from a washing machine is categorised as what kind of water in terms of recycling?

4. What is the term 'solar photovoltaic' commonly known as?

5. List five materials that are commonly used on a building site which should be recycled.

UNIT 303

Understanding the practices and procedures for overseeing and organising the work environment

When working on a site it is important for the trainee electrician to realise the need for teamwork and communication with a range of people (customers, tradespeople, the site manager, etc.) to ensure the job is done correctly and on time. Understanding how to plan and organise for the correct materials and tools to be ready for each job is also essential to the smooth running of a site.

Every electrical installation project involves the electrician working with a number of people. Even a simple job such as installing additional sockets in a domestic residence involves the electrician liaising with the customer, his supervisor/employer and the supplier. In larger installations (such as the development of a new shopping centre) the list of people working on the project will include: architects, the site manager, the contracts manager, a health and safety officer, supervisors, co-workers, other tradespeople, suppliers, manufacturers, specialist installers, and the client.

In addition to working with a range of people, the electrician has to be able to interpret job requirements, order the appropriate materials, ensure the correct tools are available, and organise the job to be completed safely, on time and in an efficient manner. As time costs money, the job has to be done right, and right first time.

This unit also links to the core theme of working safely – understanding and complying with both health and safety and employment legislation.

You will need to understand the following:

➤ the types of technical and functional information available for the installation of electrotechnical systems and equipment
➤ the procedures for supplying technical and functional information to relevant people
➤ the requirements for overseeing health and safety in the work environment
➤ the requirements for liaising with others when organising and overseeing work activities
➤ the requirements for organising and overseeing work programmes
➤ the requirements for organising the provision and storage of resources that are required for work activities

Key knowledge

➤ Understanding and sourcing technical information

➤ Communicating information to others

➤ Health and safety in the workplace

➤ Teamworking

➤ Employment law and recruitment of new staff

➤ Organising work materials

In this unit you will be given a project scenario and will use your skills to identify the appropriate answers. The project will develop as you work through the unit, with additional information given as you progress through the activities.

Project scenario

You work as a JIB-registered electrician for Swayburn Electrics Ltd, a family-owned company which has been operating for 35 years. The business is managed by James Swayburn. It currently employs six qualified electricians (including two senior electricians, of which you are one) and has two apprentices – a total of eight electrical staff. The office manager, Rachel Swayburn, deals with all the invoicing, ordering and payroll.

Swayburn Electrics Ltd has recently won the contract for the electrical work on a major hotel refurbishment and expansion programme. The original building has been purchased by Staycation Hotels. The building needs a complete refurbishment to bring it up to current regulations and customer expectations. In addition to the refurbishment, Staycation Hotels want to convert part of the underground car park into a leisure facility, including a gym, sauna, hot tub and hair and beauty salon. The architect for the project is Joanne Greeson from Perfect Designs Ltd.

The hotel manager, Andrew Wilson, wants the hotel to open for business in six months and has already set the date for the official opening party. The site manager, Peter Dawson, has concerns that the timescale is quite tight. The work is being completed by a number of sub-contractors, each focusing on one specific trade. The plumbing is being managed by Richard Dunk of Plumbrite; the joinery by Simon Emery of Connaught Carpentry; and the general building work by Sean Murphy of Ace Masons Ltd. In addition, there are some specialist installers who will be installing the sauna and hot tub in the spa area. The recently appointed salon manager is Chardonnay Taylor. She has no experience of overseeing the creation of a new salon, reading plans or working with tradespeople.

Sourcing and communicating technical information

James Swayburn has nominated you as the senior electrician to oversee the electrical installation of the leisure complex, including the hair and beauty salon. You have one qualified electrician and one apprentice working with you. The other Swayburn electrical staff are all working on the site on the rewiring and refurbishment of the building.

In this role, you will have to work with a variety of people. Complete the table below, outlining what relationship each person has to you (supervisor, customer, etc.) and what information you may need to provide them with.

Person	Relationship	What do they expect from you?	What information will you need to provide them with?
James Swayburn	My employer and senior manager who has full responsibility for overseeing the electrical installations for this contract.	Work to be completed on time, compliant with all relevant regulations and within budget.	Regular updates on the progress of the work and the real and budgeted costings. Identification and reporting of any problems. Time sheets for staff, requirements for variations.
Joanne Greeson			
Andrew Wilson			
Peter Dawson			
Chardonnay Taylor			
Apprentice electrician			
Electrician			

Person	Relationship	What do they expect from you?	What information will you need to provide them with?
Richard Dunk			
Simon Emery			
Sean Murphy			
Local electrical wholesaler			

Supplying technical information

ACTIVITY

Rachel Swayburn contacts you and asks you to get the best price for the electrical cables for this job, as the current supplier's prices have doubled since the initial quote was put in for the contract. Rachel is not technically qualified, so does not understand the importance of ensuring the correct cable is selected for each of the different circuits.

You know the hair and beauty development includes a kitchen area, sauna, hot tub, laundry area, an area for cutting and styling and two sunbeds, as well as multiple lighting circuits.

Looking at the leisure complex plan, you will need to identify the types of cables you need.

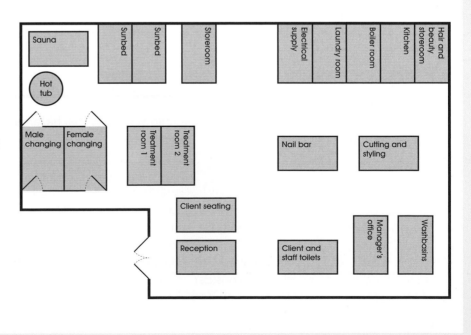

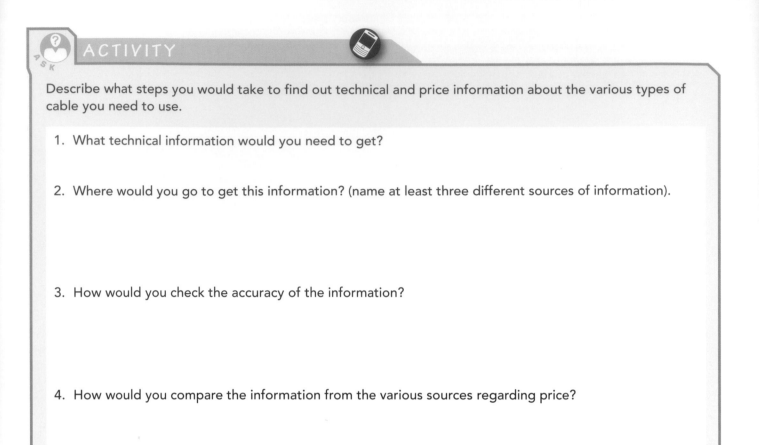

ACTIVITY

Describe what steps you would take to find out technical and price information about the various types of cable you need to use.

1. What technical information would you need to get?

2. Where would you go to get this information? (name at least three different sources of information).

3. How would you check the accuracy of the information?

4. How would you compare the information from the various sources regarding price?

key terms

Risk assessment
a procedure that identifies potential risk of harm to people on the site. It is a legal requirement.

Overseeing health and safety in the workplace

Peter Dawson, the site manager, has asked all of the senior contractors to respond to the recent **risk assessments** the health and safety officer had compiled for the site. Businesses have to assess any potential dangers and identify what steps they will take to reduce the risk of harm to workers and visitors to the site.

ACTIVITY

The health and safety officer has identified the following potential hazards in his draft report. You are required to complete the table.

Identify the hazards	Who might be harmed and how?	What are you already doing?	What further action is necessary?	How will you put the assessment into action?
Spot hazards by walking around the workplace, asking co-workers what they think, checking manufacturers instructions.	Identify groups of people who may be at risk. Some workers have particular needs. Also consider visitors and members of the public.	List what is already in place to reduce the likelihood of harm or make harm less serious.	What additional steps do you need to put in place to reduce potential risks.	Action by whom, timescale and when completed. Remember to prioritise and deal with high risk hazards first.

Identify the hazards	Who might be harmed and how?	What are you already doing?	What further action is necessary?	How will you put the assessment into action?
Manual handling. Includes lifting, lowering, pushing, pulling and carrying of tools, materials and equipment.				
Slips, trips and falls. The hair and beauty facility is located underground, with access via concrete stairs leading to the basement. Risk of falls from ladders when working at height. Trip hazards from poorly stored materials and equipment.				
Electrocution risk from portable power tools. Risks from working with live circuits. Particular concerns over risks where electrical cables are near water pipes.				
Working with moving equipment. Refurbishment work involves the movement of forklift trucks, cherry pickers and delivery vehicles.				
Inadequate lighting. The current underground car park has no external windows and therefore no natural light.				
Exposure to asbestos. Removal of old ceiling and wall partitioning. Removal of old electrical distribution units.				

Identify the hazards	Who might be harmed and how?	What are you already doing?	What further action is necessary?	How will you put the assessment into action?
Work-related stress. Timescales for completing the refurbishment are tight, so there are long hours, overtime and shorter breaks.				
Lack of communication between tradespeople. Some workers may have poor English-language skills. Planning and scheduling of work without adequate consultation between trades.				

You are also required to produce a method statement regarding the safe and secure storage of the electrical tools and materials that will be used on the site. Complete the proforma below.

Method statement for the secure storage of electrical equipment

Job	Staycation Hotel refurbishment contract
Method statement number	Version 1
Date	
Written by	

Description of works

Task	Safe storage and use of materials and equipment during the development of the hair and beauty facility within the Staycation Hotel complex.
Duration	
Sequence of work	
Location	

Resources and materials involved

Plant and equipment	
Materials (including approximate weight)	

Personal protective equipment

Equipment required by law	
Equipment required by risk assessment	

Emergency arrangements

Evacuation	
Rescue	
First aid	

Communication routes

Information for changing requirements goes to	

Staff briefing on method statement

Name	Organisation	Signature

Working with others and overseeing work programmes

Work has now begun on the development. The main building work for the creation of the underground leisure and hair and beauty salon has been completed. You are now at the first fix phase for electrics and plumbing. There are a number of areas that involve close communication with Plumbrite staff in order to plan the electrical installation work (the laundry room, sauna, hot tub, boiler room and changing rooms.)

You have decided to arrange a meeting with Richard Dunk to agree how both contractors' staff will work together to ensure the smooth and timely completion of the first fix.

ACTIVITY

Draw up an agenda for the meeting. Outline the key topics you need to discuss with Richard regarding the first fix. The agenda should include: time, location and date of meeting, who will be attending, items to discuss, AOB (any other business), health and safety and a progress report.

Work has started on the first fix. Unfortunately, the electrician working with you had a nasty fall while working on a ladder installing the lighting circuits. He broke his ankle and is in a plaster cast and on crutches. He will be off work for several weeks. This is a major concern for you as the timescale to complete the work is very tight.

You ask James Swayburn if one of the other Swayburn electricians working on the site could be redeployed to work with you. Unfortunately, this is not possible due to the demands of the refurbishment in the rest of the hotel and their own tight timescales.

James asks you to complete the **accident report** for the incident and to liaise with the health and safety officer.

key terms

Accident report a written account of an accident including near misses which need to meet the requirements of the employer and Health and Safety legislation.

ACTIVITY

Complete the accident report.

Health and Safety at Work etc Act 1974 [?]
The Reporting of Injuries, Diseases and Dangerous Occurrences Regulations 1995

HSE
Health & Safety
Executive

Click here for report guidance

Report of an injury or dangerous occurrence

Filling in this form
This form must be filled in by an employer or other responsible person.

Part A

About you

1 What is your full name?

2 What is your job title?

3 What is your telephone number?

About your organisation

4 What is the name of your organisation?

5 What is its address and postcode?

6 What type of work does the organisation do?

Part B

About the incident

1 On what date did the incident happen?

2 At what time did the incident happen?
(Please use the 24-hour clock eg 0600)

3 Did the incident happen at the above address?

Yes ☐ Go to question 4

No ☐ Where did the incident happen?

☐ elsewhere in your organisation – give the
name, address and postcode

☐ at someone else's premises – give the
name, address and postcode

☐ in a public place – give details of where it
happened

If you do not know the postcode, what is
the name of the local authority?

4 In which department, or where on the premises,
did the incident happen?

F2508 (05.00)

Part C

About the injured person

If you are reporting a dangerous occurrence, go
to Part F. If more than one person was injured in the
same incident, please attach the details asked for in Part
C and Part D for each injured person.

1 What is their full name?

2 What is their home address and postcode?

3 What is their home phone number?

4 How old are they?

5 Are they

☐ male?

☐ female?

6 What is their job title?

7 Was the injured person (tick only one box)

☐ one of your employees?

☐ on a training scheme? Give details:

☐ on work experience?

☐ employed by someone else? Give details of the
employer:

☐ self-employed and at work?

☐ a member of the public?

Part D

About the injury

1 What was the injury? (eg fracture, laceration)

2 What part of the body was injured?

Next Page

3 Was the injury (tick the one box that applies)

- ☐ a fatality?
- ☐ a major injury or condition? (see accompanying notes)
- ☐ an injury to an employee or self-employed person which prevented them doing their normal work for more than 3 days?
- ☐ an injury to a member of the public which meant they had to be taken from the scene of the accident to a hospital for treatment?

4 Did the injured person (tick all the boxes that apply)

- ☐ become unconscious?
- ☐ need resuscitation?
- ☐ remain in hospital for more than 24 hours?
- ☐ none of the above.

Part E

About the kind of accident

Please tick the one box that best describes what happened, then go to Part G.

- ☐ Contact with moving machinery or material being machined
- ☐ Hit by a moving, flying or falling object
- ☐ Hit by a moving vehicle
- ☐ Hit something fixed or stationary

- ☐ Injured while handling, lifting or carrying
- ☐ Slipped, tripped or fell on the same level
- ☐ Fell from a height
  How high was the fall?

  | metres |

- ☐ Trapped by something collapsing

- ☐ Drowned or asphyxiated
- ☐ Exposed to, or in contact with, a harmful substance
- ☐ Exposed to fire
- ☐ Exposed to an explosion

- ☐ Contact with electricity or an electrical discharge
- ☐ Injured by an animal
- ☐ Physically assaulted by a person

- ☐ Another kind of accident (describe it in Part G)

Part F

Dangerous occurrences

Enter the number of the dangerous occurrence you are reporting. (The numbers are given in the Regulations and in the notes which accompany this form)

Part G

Describing what happened

Give as much detail as you can. For instance

- the name of any substance involved
- the name and type of any machine involved
- the events that led to the incident
- the part played by any people.

If it was a personal injury, give details of what the person was doing. Describe any action that has since been taken to prevent a similar incident. Use a separate piece of paper if you need to.

Part H

Your signature

Signature

Date

Where to send the form

If returning by post/fax, please ensure this form is signed, alternatively, if returning by E-Mail, please type your name in the signature box

Incident Contact Centre, Caerphilly Business Centre, Caerphilly Business Park, Caerphilly, CF83 3GG. or email to riddor@connaught.plc.uk or fax to 0845 300 99 24

For official use			
Client number	Location number	Event number	
			☐ INV REP ☐ Y ☐ N

James Swayburn also asks you to draft an advert for a qualified and experienced electrician to work with you for three months until the project is completed. The advert is to go into both the local newspaper and the job centre.

ACTIVITY

Draft an advert for a qualified electrician to work with you on this project. Think about qualifications, skills, experience and salary. Would the electrician be fully employed by Swayburn Electrics Ltd or a self-employed sub-contractor? How will you check the person's competency and qualifications? Think about any relevant legislation you might have to consider when drafting the advert.

Organising and overseeing work

Your advert was successful and you managed to recruit Robert Wiseman to work with you. Robert is very experienced. In fact, he used to run his own electrical contracting company, but unfortunately his company went into administration one year ago when one of his major clients collapsed due to the impact of the recession on the construction industry. Robert has been doing some work as a jobbing electrician, but hasn't found a permanent position.

Robert is several years older than you and used to being in charge of his own staff. You have taken him on as an employee on a three-month probation period. The hope is that if Robert fits in, he could have a permanent job with the company. James seems to think the electrician with the broken leg will not be returning due to medical complications and his doctor's advice.

The apprentice, Amir Hassan, is currently completing his second year. He attends college one day per week to complete his technical qualifications and key/functional skills. You regularly meet with the assessor overseeing his NVQ to give progress reports and to confirm how well Amir is performing in the workplace. However, at the latest review meeting, you were advised that he has not been attending the college regularly. When he does attend, he has a poor attitude in the classroom. The teachers are concerned that he may fail his technical certificate. You are surprised to hear this because his attendance, punctuality, attitude and work for you has been very good.

ACTIVITY

1. How would you check that Robert experience and qualifications are true as claimed?

2. What barriers do you think Robert could have working for you?

3. How would you motivate Robert to ensure he works effectively for you on this contract?

4. How would you tackle Amir's poor attendance at college?

5. What information would you ask the college and the assessor to give you regarding Amir?

6. Is there anything you should report to James or Rachel Swayburn?

ACTIVITY

1. What is the minimum wage applicable to an apprentice under 18?

2. What is the current maximum time an employee under 18 can work legally?

3. What equal opportunities legislation applies regarding the recruitment of staff?

4. What information should be included on a pay statement?

Chardonnay has asked you to attend a meeting to discuss the lighting in the hair and beauty salon. She has seen photographs of a different salon, which have inspired her. On the original plan the lighting was simply going to be reduced-voltage spotlighting. She wants to change some of the lighting in the salon area to create 'mood zones'. Chardonnay still wants to have spotlights over the washbasin and nail bar areas, but wants lighting around the mirrors in the cutting and styling area. The mirrors are free-standing units which separate clients (one on either side); Chardonnay's vision is for a 'Hollywood hair and beauty experience' for the client. She also wants multi-coloured LED twinkling fairy lights in the ceiling above the hot tub and wall lighting around the sauna, sunbed and changing room area.

MANAGE ACTIVITY

1. How would you feel about Chardonnay's request to change the lighting at this stage?

2. What would you advise Chardonnay? What information might you need?

3. What are the implications for the materials and costs?

THINK ACTIVITY

The customer is always right! James says you have to draw up plans for the revised lighting.

Draw the appropriate lighting symbols in the correct locations on the plan.

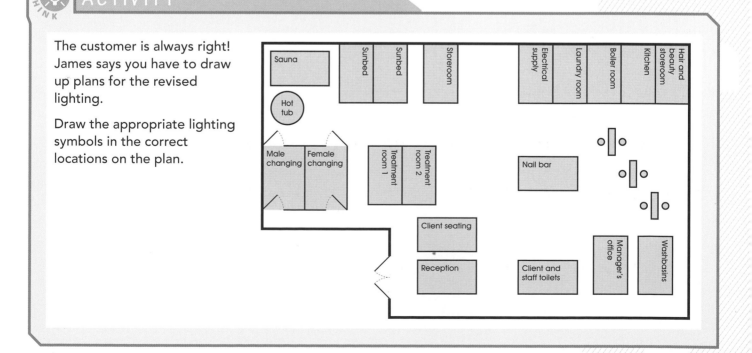

Your questions answered...

Some of my electrician co-workers seem to get into a bit of bother with management when discussing how the company works and who they do and don't like. What are the codes of conduct when working on-site and representing my employer?

You are a worker for your company and need to show a degree of loyalty to your employer. This means that certain things are not allowed:

- Do not badmouth your employer to a customer.
- Do not do 'favours' for others using company property.
- Do not speak for your employer when you have no authority.
- Never assume that you know what your employer wants. If you are unsure, ask.

However, there are certain things that you should do:

- Learn how to put people at ease.
- Develop good relationships with customers.
- Know your job – good knowledge of the relevant standards helps customer relationships, and promotes their confidence in you and your company.

Remember, you may be the reason your company gets more work from a particular client. In the end, it may be your job that is lost because of the lost contract. The customer may have some knowledge of electrical work and would be aware if they were being given the run around or ripped off.

QUICK QUIZ

HOW MUCH DO YOU KNOW ABOUT RECRUITING STAFF AND OVERSEEING WORK?

1. How would you track the budget for the job?

2. What qualifications would you expect Robert Wiseman to have before you employed him?

3. What would you do with the written job applications you receive in response to the advert?

4. What legislation would you need to take into account when recruiting new staff?

5. Who should be notified of a fall in the workplace which resulted in an electrician breaking their ankle?

UNIT 304

Understanding the principles of planning and selection for the installation of electrotechnical equipment and systems in buildings, structures and the environment

The earth can be considered to be a large conductor, which is at zero potential. The purpose of **earthing** is to connect together all metal work (other than that which is intended to carry current) to earth so dangerous potential differences cannot exist either between different metal parts, or between metal parts and earth. The definition given in BS7671 for earthing describes it as the 'act of connecting the exposed conductive parts of an installation to the main earthing terminal of that installation'.

Earthing is one of the most important factors where the safety of installations is concerned. By using the correct earthing procedures, danger to life and risk of fire to property can be greatly reduced.

key terms

Earthing the process of connecting together all metalwork to prevent dangerous potential differences between different metals or between metals and earth. Correct earthing procedures prevent danger to life and risk of fire from excessive currents.

You will need to understand the following:

➤ the characteristics and applications of consumer supply systems
➤ the principles of internal and external earthing arrangements for electrical installations for buildings, structures and the environment
➤ the principles for selecting cables and circuit protection devices
➤ the principles and procedures for selecting wiring systems, equipment and enclosures

Key knowledge

➤ Understanding consumer supply systems

➤ The purpose of earthing

➤ Protection against shock

➤ Selecting circuit protection devices

➤ Voltage drop

➤ Disconnection times

➤ Thermal constraints

➤ Choice of wiring systems

LEARNING CENTRE
NANTGARW CAMPUS
COLEG MORGANNWG

Consumer supply systems

THINK ACTIVITY

There are several earthing arrangements in consumer supply systems, as listed in the table. Complete the table.

Type of earthing system	Description of earthing arrangement, to include the details on how the earthing is provided. Include in your descriptions details about the letters I, T, N, C and S and what they mean.
TN–S	
TNC–S	
TN–C	
TT	
IT	

Purpose of earthing

By connecting to earth all metalwork not intended to carry current, a path is provided for leakage current, which can be detected and interrupted by fuses, circuit breakers and residual current devices. Figure 4.1 illustrates the earth return path from the consumer's earth to the supply earth. The connection at the consumer's earth can be by means of either an earth electrode at the building where the earth is required or may be in the form of a cable that runs back to the generator or transformer and is then connected to an earth point. Because the transformer or generator at the point of supply always has an earth point, a circuit is formed when earth fault currents are flowing. If these fault currents are large enough they will operate the protective device, thereby isolating the circuit. The **star point** of the secondary winding in a three-phase four-wire distribution transformer is connected to the earth so to maintain the neutral at earth potential.

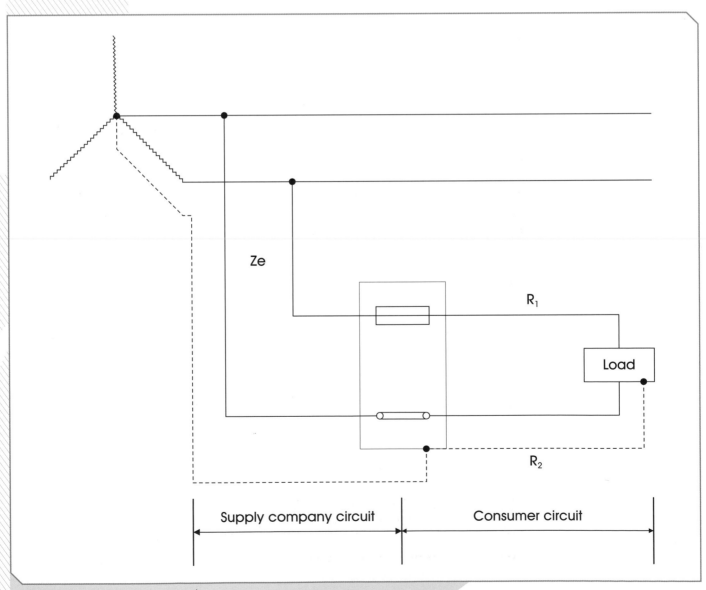

Figure 4.1: The earth return path.

ACTIVITY

Draw the line diagram for the following earthing systems. Fully label each diagram.

TN–S

TNC–S

TN–C

TT

IT

Principles of internal and external earthing

ACTIVITY

Earthing and bonding

There is a distinction between earthing and bonding. Write your definition of earthing and bonding.

Protection against shock

There are two ways a person can be at risk of electric shock:

1. **Direct contact** – touching parts of equipment or systems that are intended to be live.

2. **Indirect contact** – touching conductive parts, which are not meant to be live, but which have become live due to a fault.

ACTIVITY

Complete the table, indicating ways protection can be provided against the risks of direct and indirect contact.

Risk	Ways to provide protection
Direct contact	
Indirect contact	

It is important to understand that the majority of electrical equipment is connected directly to an REC (Regional Electric Company) supply cable. The possible fault level of such can be to the order of 16,000 amps. Therefore, any protective equipment must be able to operate at this level of current.

It is also recognised that electrical equipment is fixed equipment, as defined in BS7671 Wiring Regulations. As such, circuits should be designed to provide disconnection within five seconds of a fault occurring.

Fuses

BS1361- and BS1362-type fuses, generally termed 'cartridge fuses', have a fusible wire enclosed within a glass or ceramic tube. The purpose of the tube is to enclose the resultant arc of the fuse element under fault conditions.

There are also rewireable fuses in use, known as BS3036 fuses. These are obsolete and should be replaced with cartridge fuses or MCBs (Miniature Circuit Breakers) if encountered.

High breaking capacity fuses

BS88-type fuses, commonly referred to as high breaking capacity (HBC) fuses, are capable of breaking very heavy fault currents. Compared with the cartridge fuse, the fuse element is of better quality, the tube is of substantial ceramic construction and filled with silica sand to ensure quick arc extinction.

Circuit breakers

These are electromagnetic devices having both thermal and magnetic elements.

This combination allows for the detection of overload where the bi-metallic strip is heated and operates the trip. In the case of a fault, the higher current creates a strong magnetic field in the electromagnet, causing the trip to operate very quickly.

ACTIVITY

Draw a simple diagram of the protective devices listed. List the advantages and disadvantages of each device.

BS3036 rewireable fuse	Advantages:
	Disadvantages:
BS1361/1362 fuse	Advantages:
	Disadvantages:
BS88 fuse	Advantages:
	Disadvantages:

Cable and circuit protection device selection

Cable selection

To understand how to install electrical systems safely is a major part of an electrician's training, and requires a great deal of technical knowledge and practical skills. Achieving a good understanding of installations and the practice of installing can be difficult. Successful installation requires more than simply choosing some cable and attaching a piece of equipment to it. It requires a lot of thought combined with excellent problem-solving abilities and good technical knowledge.

There are many things to consider during installation, such as:

➤ The *temperature* in which the wiring will operate.

➤ The *environment* in which the electrical installation will operate.

➤ The *energy rating* of the equipment or system to be installed.

➤ The capacity of the *wiring* or *cabling*.

➤ Which *protective device* to use.

➤ Correctly calculating the *load*.

ACTIVITY

The symbols in the table relate to details from the BS7671 IEE Regulations. Match up the symbol with its description with arrows.

Symbol	Description
Ib	The nominal line voltage to earth
It	The ratio of the kW (true power) to the kVA (apparent power)
Uo	The normal load current in a circuit
Ca	The current rating or setting of the protective device (this could be a fuse or MCB)
Cg	When any correction factors have been applied we have a value for the effective current carrying capacity of the conductor
PF	The value of current found by applying the Iz to the current carrying capacity
In	A factor applied to cables when the ambient temperature needs to be taken into account
Iz	A factor applied to the cable when two or more cables are run close together
Mi	The correction factor applied to cables that are protected by a semi-enclosed fuse. The factor is 0.725
Ct	A correction factor applied to the cable when it has thermal insulation on one side of the cable only or is totally surrounded by thermal insulation
Cc	A factor that is only applied to certain cable types. The factor is 0.9
Ci	The rating factor for the operating temperature of the cable

➤ Routing the cabling or wiring correctly.

➤ Ensuring the installation is *wired properly*.

➤ Ensuring *voltage drop* requirements are met.

➤ Ensuring adequate *shock protection* is provided for.

➤ Ensuring the application of *diversity factors*, if applicable.

All these things are extremely important: inaccurate calculations and poor installation could lead to overloads, fire and personal injury.

Voltage drop

The resistance of the conductor becomes greater as the length of the cable increases or the cross-sectional area of the cable is reduced. This means that on long cable runs, to have the benefit of declared voltage, the cable cross-sectional area may have to be increased, thus reducing the resistance and allowing more current to 'flow'.

It is important in cable selection to calculate the length of cable run and permissible voltage drop for the load being supplied. Regulation 525 states that in the absence of any other considerations, under normal conditions the requirements for voltage drop must comply with those stated in Table 12A in Appendix 12 of the IEE regulations (BS7671).

ACTIVITY

Referring to Table 12A in Appendix 12 of the IEE regulations book, complete the table, filling in the missing values. Write a description, in your own words, of what is meant by the various definitions.

Voltage drop		
Information	Lighting	Other use

The following formula should be used when calculating the actual voltage drop:

$$\text{voltage drop (VD)} = \frac{\text{mV/A} \times \text{Ib} \times \text{L}}{1{,}000}$$

ACTIVITY

A circuit is to supply a load of 2.75 kW at 230 V and 50 Hz. A PVC-insulated and sheathed, steel-wire armoured cable is to be installed, clipped to a perforated metal cable tray, with a total cable length of 30 m from the distribution board. The distribution board is located at the supply intake position. For most of its length, the cable is installed touching two other cables in an ambient temperature of 45 °C. If protection is by a BS88-type fuse and the voltage drop must not exceed that stated in Table 12A, what is the minimum size of cable that can be used to comply with both current carrying capacity and voltage drop constraints? Show all your calculations.

Circuit disconnection times

key terms

Shock protection
protection against direct and indirect contact to prevent humans or livestock suffering from electric shock. Provided by barriers, covers, insulation, fuses, MCBs, RCDs and effective earthing.

It is necessary to check the circuit for **shock protection**. In other words, will the protective device that has been chosen to protect the circuit operate within the specified time limits in the event of a fault?

The speed of operation of the protective device is extremely important and will depend on the size of the fault current. This, in turn, will depend on the impedance of the earth fault loop path.

The formula for calculating shock protection is

$$\text{Actual } Zs = Ze + \frac{(\{R_1 + R_2\} \times \text{multiplier} \times \text{length}) \text{ ohms}}{1000}$$

ACTIVITY

An electric cooking appliance is to be installed in commercial premises. The circuit is wired using a 12 m length of 6.0 mm² PVC-sheathed cable clipped direct to a surface, and containing 2.5 mm² CPC. A 45 A BS1361 cartridge fuse protects the circuit. The value of Ze for the installation is given as 0.40 Ω. Assuming that there are no correction factors for grouping or ambient temperature, determine whether the circuit complies with BS7671 for shock protection. The nominal voltage may be taken as 230 V and the design current is 45 A. Show all your calculations.

Thermal constraints

The purpose of this element of cable selection is to check that the earth cable (CPC) is large enough in CSA (Cross Sectional Area) to safely carry the fault current without damage to the cable.

This can be verified in two ways:

1. Refer to the correct tables in BS7671.

2. Use the adiabatic calculation.

The adiabatic equation is:

$$S = \frac{\sqrt{I_{ef}^2 \times t}}{k}$$

where:

S = the cross-sectional area of the CPC in mm²

I_{ef} = the value of the fault current I_{ef} for earth fault current

t = the operating time of the disconnecting device in seconds

k = a factor depending on the conductor and its insulating material.

ACTIVITY

A BS88 fuse protects a 20 A radial socket outlet circuit. The circuit is wired using 2.5 mm² single core cable installed in a 16 m length of PVC conduit. A separate protective conductor consisting of a 1.0 mm² PVC cable is used. Assuming that no correction factors are applicable and that the value of Ze is given as 0.5 Ω, determine whether the circuit complies with BS7671 for thermal constraints. The nominal voltage (Uo) may be taken as 230 volts.

I_b = 20 A
I_n = 20 A.

Show all your calculations.

Choice of wiring systems

Working in small groups, discuss and decide upon the best type of cable and enclosure to be used for the following circuits. Give a reason for your choice.

Type of circuit	Type of cable	Type of enclosure	Reason for choice
Lighting systems	Multi-core PVC sheath and PVC insulation	None required in domestic premises, but if single-core is used then PVC or steel conduit	Multi-core and single PVC is cheap and reliable
Power systems (final circuits)			
Distribution sub-mains systems			
Environmental control and building control systems			
Emergency management systems			
Security systems – fire alarms			
Security systems – unlawful entry			
Security systems – emergency lighting			
Closed-circuit television (CCTV)			
Communication and data systems			

Your questions answered...

At college I was taught the theory about the earth fault loop impedance path, but I don't understand what it means. Can you explain?

A good earth path (that is, a low resistance one) will allow a high current to flow, and this will cause the protective device to operate, thereby isolating the circuit and giving protection against electric shock.

The earth fault loop comprises:

- The circuit protective conductor (within the installation).
- The consumer's earthing terminal and earthing conductor.
- The earth return path, which can be either by means of an electrode or via the cable armouring sheath.
- The path through the earthed neutral point of the transformer and the transformer winding (or generator winding).
- The phase conductor.

The diagram illustrates this complete path.

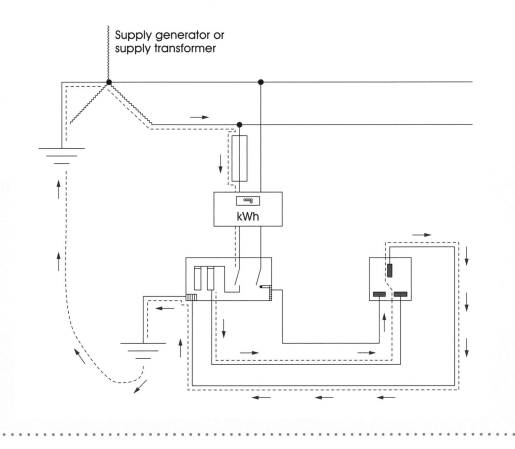

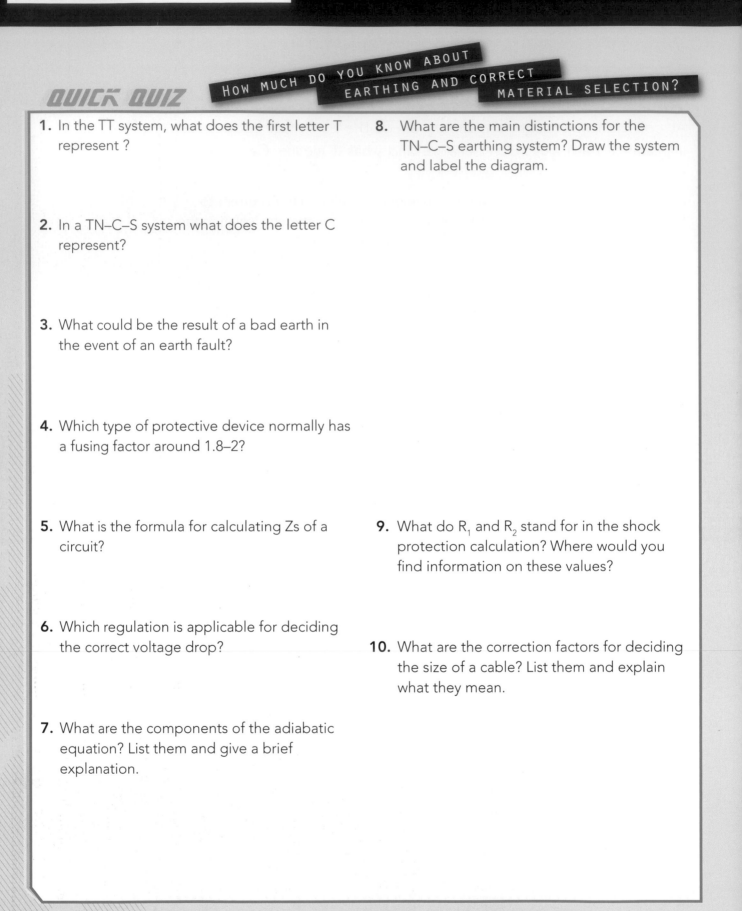

HOW MUCH DO YOU KNOW ABOUT EARTHING AND CORRECT MATERIAL SELECTION?

1. In the TT system, what does the first letter T represent ?

2. In a TN–C–S system what does the letter C represent?

3. What could be the result of a bad earth in the event of an earth fault?

4. Which type of protective device normally has a fusing factor around 1.8–2?

5. What is the formula for calculating Zs of a circuit?

6. Which regulation is applicable for deciding the correct voltage drop?

7. What are the components of the adiabatic equation? List them and give a brief explanation.

8. What are the main distinctions for the TN–C–S earthing system? Draw the system and label the diagram.

9. What do R_1 and R_2 stand for in the shock protection calculation? Where would you find information on these values?

10. What are the correction factors for deciding the size of a cable? List them and explain what they mean.

UNIT 305

Understanding the practices and procedures for the preparation and installation of wiring systems and electrotechnical equipment in buildings, structures and the environment

This unit is about making sure trainee electricians are aware of the necessary procedures when working on-site. This includes checking the work site for health and safety issues prior to starting the job. The aim is to ensure that all electricians work safely and legally to standard procedures, and that they are aware of the correct equipment and resources to use for any electrical installation.

The activities for this unit relate to the development of the Staycation Hotel, outlined in Unit 303.

You will need to understand the following:
- the procedures, practices and statutory and non-statutory regulatory requirements for preparing work sites for the installation of wiring systems and associated equipment
- the procedures for checking the work location prior to the commencement of work activities
- the practices, procedures and regulatory requirements for completing the safe isolation of electrical circuits and complete electrical installation
- the types, applications and limitations of wiring systems and associated equipment
- the procedures for selecting and using tools, equipment and fixings for the installation of wiring systems, associated equipment and enclosures
- the practices and procedures for installing wiring systems, associated equipment and enclosures
- the regulatory requirements which apply to the installation of wiring systems, associated equipment and enclosures

Key knowledge

➤ Understand site health and safety

➤ Identify/survey work sites for damage and hazards prior to work commencing

➤ Identify correct tools and materials to use

➤ Correct installation methods

➤ Know IEE regulations

➤ Know the use of different types of cables and enclosures

➤ Know correct installation methods

Project scenario

This scenario continues from the Staycation Hotel development project first introduced in Unit 303. You may need to refer back to this unit to remind you of the key personnel and the work scenario.

You are about to start the first fix on the hair and beauty salon within the complex. You and Richard Dunk from Plumbrite are doing a pre-installation inspection of the work and need to agree the schedule of work for the electricians and plumbers.

The salon is located in the basement, in what was part of an underground car park. Your first concern is the safe access and egress to the work site for the tradesmen. Currently, the main access is from the reception area of the hotel, then down concrete stairs. From the stairs you enter into what will be the hair and beauty reception area. There is no alternative access point. The underground car park was lit by fluorescent lighting, which is still installed and working. The fittings and cables all need to be removed. The floor is a concrete base. There are existing secure rooms containing the electricity supply and the boiler. These rooms are to remain in use in their current location, but will require electrical rewiring and upgrading to blend in with the rest of the build.

ACTIVITY

Work in pairs. One of you is to assume the role of the plumber. You need to do a virtual survey of the car park and associated buildings based on the plan. You need to complete the table. Think about:

- existing damage that may be apparent to the fabric of the walls and floors, to equipment and components you may have to remove, and building decor.
- the protocol to establish for access and egress to the basement.
- any other health and safety issues.

Issues found by you and Richard Dunk	Your agreed solutions
Safe storage of tools, materials, equipment and components on the site after normal working hours.	
Safe storage of materials, tools, etc. in off-site locations.	
There are several unidentified metal barrels (which you suspect contain chemicals used in vehicles) in the former car park.	
Removal and safe disposal of existing fluorescent lighting. There is no natural light in the basement.	
What access equipment will be needed to remove the existing lighting?	
What equipment do you need and how will you arrange the removal of the metal barrels?	

ACTIVITY

1. What are the legal requirements for providing a safe fire evacuation procedure in the workplace?

2. How does COSHH affect your planning before your team starts work on an electrical installation?

Rachel Swayburn has asked you to finalise the list of materials needed from the electrical wholesaler. She is aware that Chardonnay has requested some changes to the original specification but is unsure of what she needs to order.

You are to compile the list of materials required for the hair and beauty salon, taking into account the items shown in the table and Chardonnay's request for mood lighting. Remember to take into account the zonal requirements for the sauna, basins and hot tub areas.

There are two parts to this activity. Part A is to list your requirements; in Part B you have to justify your choice of materials.

Part A

Area	List of materials required
Reception	Dado trunking Socket outlets for computer, fax machine, printer, telephone switchboard and photocopier PVC single-core cables Data cabling Ceiling lighting and control
Sauna	
Hot tub	
Changing rooms	
Sunbed rooms	
Manager's office	
Cutting/styling room	
Kitchen	

Part B

Item	Will use ☑	Will not use ☒	Explanation of where these will be used and why you have selected them. You should also consider the environmental factors you need to address (for example, the sauna ambient temperature and effects of moisture on cables and insulation).
Single-core PVC cables			
Multi-core PVC cables			
Thermosetting insulated cables			
MICC (PVC-sheathed)			
MICC (without PVC sheath)			
SWA cables (PILC)			
SWA cables (XLPE)			
SWA cables (PVC)			
Flexible cables and cords			
Fire-resistant cable (FP200)			
Data cables			
Fibre-optic cables			
PVC conduit and trunking			

Item	Will use ☑	Will not use ☒	Explanation of where these will be used and why you have selected them. You should also consider the environmental factors you need to address (for example, the sauna ambient temperature and effects of moisture on cables and insulation).
Metallic conduit and trunking			
Cable tray			
Cable basket			
Ladder systems			
Ducting			
Modular wiring systems			
Busbar systems and power track			

ACTIVITY

The apprentice, Amir, has been told by his assessor he needs to get some workplace evidence to help him complete his NVQ. The area he needs to get evidence for is selecting the correct tools to use for a job. He has asked you for some advice on how he can generate the evidence usefully.

You ask him to complete the following tool guide to make sure he brings the correct equipment for the various jobs listed. Now complete this table yourself.

Tool	Item is used for ...	What checks do you need to perform before using this tool?
Electric power drill		
Electric heat gun		

Tool	Item is used for ...	What checks do you need to perform before using this tool?
230/110 volt transformer		
Angle grinder		
Battery drill		
Side cutters		
Combination pliers		
Cable-stripping pliers		
Assorted screwdrivers		
Crimping tool		

Tool	Item is used for ...	What checks do you need to perform before using this tool?
Claw hammer		
Pincers		
Pocket knife		
Hacksaw		

ACTIVITY

As the senior electrician, you need to ensure your electrician and apprentice have access to information about how to do the job. As you are not always available for them to ask you face-to-face, you have decided to write some instruction cards for the apprentice to follow if you are not available. The area the apprentice will be working on is the reception area.

For each situation, you need to write instructions on the correct procedure for fixing and installing the wiring systems, enclosures and associated electrical equipment.

Reception area – job details	Instructions to apprentice
Securing the spotlights to the ceiling	Materials needed: Tools needed: Instructions:

Reception area – job details	Instructions to apprentice
Securing multi-compartmental trunking	Materials needed: Tools needed: Instructions:
Installing an external security camera to view reception entrance and exit	Materials needed: Tools needed: Instructions:
Installing PIRs in the reception area leading to the toilets	Materials needed: Tools needed: Instructions:

ACTIVITY

As this is the first time you have had responsibility for a large project, you are a little unsure about some technical details relevant to the job. You ask your boss (a more experienced electrician), James Swayburn, for some help. James is too busy to answer you, but he suggests you look up the appropriate regulations, using the internet or any other source, relating to the following situations and make your own notes.

Systems, equipment and enclosures	IEE regulation number and explanation
Isolation and switching	
Protection against fire	
Protection against electric shock	
Special locations	
Segregation	
Flammable/explosive atmospheres	

I understand that when installing a sauna there are three identified zones. What are the differences between the zones?

You are correct, there are three zones in a room containing a sauna. Information can be found in Section 703 of the IIE regulations.

In summary, Zone 1 is the area that contains the sauna heater – see the diagram.

ELEVATION

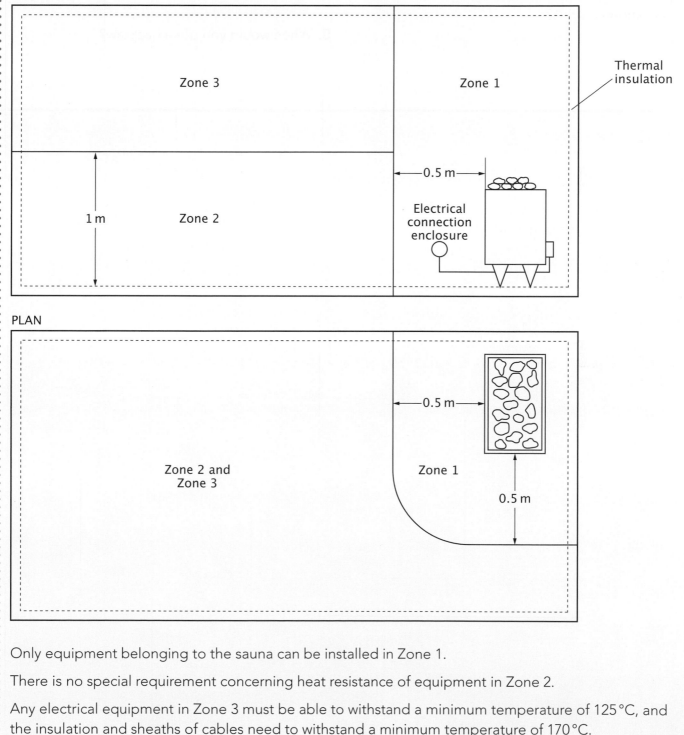

Only equipment belonging to the sauna can be installed in Zone 1.

There is no special requirement concerning heat resistance of equipment in Zone 2.

Any electrical equipment in Zone 3 must be able to withstand a minimum temperature of 125°C, and the insulation and sheaths of cables need to withstand a minimum temperature of 170°C.

QUICK QUIZ

HOW MUCH DO YOU KNOW ABOUT THE SAFE USE OF EQUIPMENT?

1. What tool would you use for stripping the plastic covering off electrical cable?

2. Employers have a legal responsibility to make sure all portable electrical equipment is safe to use. What is the regulation which stipulates this?

3. How frequently should portable appliances be tested?

4. When would you use SWA cables (XLPE)?

5. When would you use a hacksaw?

UNIT 306

Understanding the principles, practices and legislation for the termination and connection of conductors, cables and cords in electrical systems

This unit links closely with Units 305, 307 and 308. Some of the learning outcomes overlap; these will be covered in the following units.

There is now an extensive range of cables and flexible cords that all need terminating and connecting in a safe and secure way. It is important that these connections are correctly performed as otherwise they can pose a risk of damage to property, injury or even death! Poorly connected joints can lead to excessive heat, which can lead to fire and/or electric shock.

You will need to understand the following:

➤ the principles, regulatory requirements and procedures for completing the safe isolation of electrical circuits and complete installations

➤ the regulatory requirements and procedures for terminating and connecting conductors, cables and flexible cords in electrical wiring systems and equipment

➤ the procedures and applications of different methods of terminating and connecting conductors, cables and flexible cords in electrical wiring systems and equipment

Key knowledge

➤ Sources of relevant technical and legal information

➤ A range of different wiring systems

➤ A range of different electrical equipment

➤ Different methods of connecting wiring systems

➤ Health and safety requirements (including PPE and risk assessment)

Different wiring systems

ACTIVITY

The table lists all the different types of electrical wiring systems you may have to connect and terminate. Select the most appropriate method by ticking the relevant column, then justifying your choice. If there is more than one correct method, write 1, 2, 3 or 4 in the appropriate columns in preferential order.

	Screw connection	Crimped connection	Soldered connection	A non-screw compression connection	Justify your choice
PVC single-core					
PVC multi-core					
MICC					
SWA (PVC)					
SWA (XLPE)					
SWA (PILC)					
Armoured flexible cables					
Braided flexible cords					
Thermosetting insulated cables					
Data cables					
Fibre-optic cables					

Electrical connections and terminations

ACTIVITY

In the table, draw a diagram of an electrical **connection** or termination. Choose four different cable types from the previous table. There is an example of a pillar terminal connection shown below. Your drawing should include the relevant cables.

Cable and connection type	Diagram
Pillar terminal	
Screw connection	
Crimped connection	
Soldered connection/joint	
Non-screw compression joint	

key terms

Connection a joint in non-flexible cables, which should be soldered, brazed, welded or made using mechanical clamps or with a compression joint.

Your questions answered...

Why does my supervisor keep on at me to check that all the termination and connections I make are screwed tightly? Also, he asks me to check that I haven't connected an aluminium conductor onto a steel or copper conductor. Why is that important?

It is really important that any screwed connections are tight, as loose joints can lead to a high-resistance joint. High-resistance joints can cause a significant rise in temperature and possibly fire.

If two dissimilar metals are touching one another in a damp environment, corrosion could occur because of an electrolytic attack. This means the decomposition/corrosion of the metals touching each other when an electric current flows through them. The joint would become unsafe, and could lead to a fire or electric shock.

QUICK QUIZ

1. What is the main function of the sheathing on cables and flexes?
   a. Provides identification.
   b. Provides mechanical protection.
   c. Provides colour coding.
   d. Provides a CPC.

2. The abbreviation CPC stands for?
   a. Circuit phase conductor.
   b. Critical path conductor.
   c. Continuity protective conductor.
   d. Circuit protective conductor.

3. The manufacturer's code ref 6491 X refers to which type of cable?
   a. Steel wire armoured (SWA).
   b. Mineral insulated (MICC).
   c. Multi-core (PVC).
   d. Single-core (PVC).

4. What is the maximum continuous operating temperature for XLPE-type cable?
   a. 70 °C
   b. 80 °C
   c. 90 °C
   d. 100 °C

UNIT 307

Understanding principles, practices and legislation for the inspection, testing, commissioning and certification of electrotechnical systems and equipment in buildings, structures and the environments

Before you can commence inspection or testing of installations, machines and equipment there are certain things, which must be checked. It is essential that the person carrying out the inspection and testing (electrician or apprentice) is competent. The inspector must be experienced and must also be sufficiently knowledgeable of the type of installation and machines that are to be inspected and tested to ensure no danger is caused to any person, livestock or property.

You will need to understand the following:

➤ the principles, regulatory requirements and procedures for completing the safe isolation of an electrical circuit and complete electrical installations in preparation for inspection, testing and commissioning

➤ the principles and regulatory requirements for inspecting, testing and commissioning electrical systems, equipment and components

➤ the regulatory requirements and procedures for completing the inspection of electrical installations

➤ the regulatory requirements and procedures for the safe testing and commissioning of electrical installations

➤ the procedures and requirements for the completion of electrical installation certificates and related documentation

Prior to carrying out an inspection and test the inspector must be aware of:

➤ the maximum demand expressed in amperes.

➤ the number and type of live conductors, the source of energy and the circuits used in the installation.

➤ the type of earthing arrangement used by the installation and any facilities provided by the supplier for the user.

The person carrying out the inspection must also be aware of the following design criteria in respect of the installation to be inspected. The Health and Safety at Work Act and Electricity at Work Regulations 1989 also require this.

➤ The type and composition of circuits, including points of utilisation, number and size of conductors and type of cable.

➤ A description and the location of devices performing the functions of protection and isolation.

➤ The method selected to prevent danger from shock in the event of an earth fault.

➤ Any circuit or equipment vulnerable to a particular test should be identified.

Electrical installations should be designed into separate circuits (for example, power, lighting, cooker circuits) to avoid danger in the event of faults and to facilitate the safe operation of the inspection and testing process.

After inspection and testing, the record of results (or certificate) forms a legal document. The person carrying out the inspection is personally liable to make sure the tests have been completed correctly and the information recorded accurately using the following documentation:

➤ Electrical Installation Certificate

➤ Schedule of Inspections

➤ Schedule of Test Results

➤ Minor Electrical Installation Works Certificate.

Key knowledge

➤ Safe isolation of circuits and installations

➤ Inspecting and testing

➤ Regulatory requirements

➤ Certificates and record keeping

Project scenario

This scenario continues the Staycation Hotel project first introduced in Unit 303. You may need to refer back to this unit to remind you of the key personnel and the work scenario.

Understanding the requirements for the inspection of an installation

You, Robert and Amir have been working hard and the installation of the electrical systems is now complete. Amir has recently had a visit from his assessor. In order to complete his NVQ qualification he needs to gather evidence of inspecting and testing. At the review meeting, you have agreed, with the assessor, to allow Amir to carry out the inspection, testing and certification of a number of installations in the hair and beauty salon.

ACTIVITY

The first phase of the inspection is to be a site walkabout, with yourself and Amir, to carry out an initial verification and inspection of the installation. During the walkabout, you ask Amir to explain what he is looking for.

1. What would you be looking for when undertaking a visual inspection? Think about the materials used, checking for damage and compliance with regulations.

2. In relation to the hot tub, what in particular should you be looking out for?

3. In relation to the data cabling in the office and reception areas, what would you be checking for?

ACTIVITY

One of the other hotels in the Staycation chain has recently had to close its leisure facility due to a health and safety incident. A hotel client was leaning out from the shower cubicle to reach for a towel from the electric towel rail, and received a severe electric shock. This accident was reported to the Health and Safety Executive, who insisted on a full inspection of the hotel's electrical installation. The inspection showed that the towel rail had not been earthed. There was a lot of bad publicity for this hotel, and it had a knock-on effect for the other hotels in the chain.

The hotel manager has contacted James Swayburn to stress the importance of this incident never happening again. James has assured him that all circuits will be correctly installed and tested, with particular emphasis on any wet areas.

James has now asked you to compile a chart outlining what earthing and bonding systems have been installed and to justify the reason for the selection.

Complete the chart. You should tick the appropriate columns for your choice of earthing or bonding requirements. You then need to explain your reason for selecting that method.

Area	Earthing conductors	Circuit protective conductors	Main bonding conductors	Supplementary bonding conductors	Isolation	Type and rating of overcurrent protective devices	Justify your reason for selection
Hot tub							
Sauna							
Laundry							
Kitchen							
Electrical supply room							

ACTIVITY

Testing the installation: a two-stage activity

Stage 1: the table shows the 12 tests that can be carried out while testing an installation. Write a number at the side of each test to indicate the correct sequence in which the tests must be carried out. The first one has already been completed

Test	Sequence number
Check of phase sequence	
Protection by separation of circuits	
Continuity of all protective conductors	1
Earth fault loop impedance	
Continuity of ring final circuit conductors	
Insulation resistance/impedance floors and walls	
Functional testing	
Prospective fault current	
Polarity	
Earth electrode resistance	
Basic protection by barriers and enclosures provided during erection	
Insulation resistance	

Stage 2: once you have identified the correct order, write the tests in the following table in the correct sequence. The right-hand column lists the positive outcomes from the tests, but they are not in the correct order. You need to identify which outcome relates to each test and draw an arrow between them.

Test number from above	Expected outcome if test was carried out correctly
1 Continuity of all protective conductors tested OK	Ring circuit is complete with no interconnections. CPC (Circuit Protective Conductor) is sound and correctly sized for prospective fault currents.
2	Overcurrent protective devices must, under earth fault conditions, disconnect fast enough to reduce the risk of electric shock. Earth fault loop resistance must be low enough for this to happen.
3	Floors and walls are found to be non-conductive. No risk of electric shock to human beings or livestock.
4	The PSCC (Prospective Short Circuit Current) has been determined and has been taken into full account in the system's design. The electrical installation is safe – protective devices operate correctly under fault conditions.
5	The resistance of the main and supplementary conductors are acceptable values. Continuity of CPC in final circuits is found to be sound.
6	Table 61 of BS7671 is used to find the correct test values for circuits operating at different voltages. SELV (Separated Extra Low Voltage) and PELV (Protected Extra Low Voltage) circuits are found to be separated from other voltage circuits.

Test number from above	Expected outcome if test was carried out correctly
7	Earth electrode resistance does NOT exceed BS7671 maximum. The electrical installation is safe and earth fault currents are safely passed to earth.
8	Site fabricated enclosures and barriers are safe and have the correct IP ratings. The temporary/construction site installation is safe to use.
9	RCDs/RCBOs operate in the correct time interval and at the set value of leakage current. Switch gear, control gear, interlocks, etc. function correctly.
10	Switches, lamp-holders and socket outlets are wired correctly. Line conductor is isolated when switches are in off position.
11	Insulation resistance is found to be in excess of minimum value required by BS7671. Installation is safe to use.
12	A phase rotation meter is used to verify that the correct phase sequence has been maintained.

ACTIVITY

You have been asked to show Amir how to carry out a number of tests. In the spaces below, write a description of how this test is carried out. Include diagrams to illustrate your answer

Test	Description	Diagram
Insulation resistance		
Continuity of circuit protective conductors		
Polarity		
Automatic disconnection of the supply		
Correct operation of RCDs		

ACTIVITY

The work has now been completed, tested and inspected and must be certificated. Amir needs to produce evidence of being competent in completing certification. You want to double-check his knowledge before allowing him to complete the certificate. Certificates are legal documents, so it is really important that everything is done correctly. You need to make sure Amir understands the different documents involved in recording electrical installation works and what each document covers. Before questioning him, you decide to devise a crib sheet which will help you check his answers.

Complete the table to use as an answer guide when questioning Amir.

Document	Explain the purpose	What information must be included	Who needs copies of the certificates
An Electrical Installation Certificate (form 1)			
Schedule of Inspections			
Schedule of Test Results			
A Minor Electrical Installation Works Certificate			

ACTIVITY

Amir has now completed his first test schedule and hands it to you for checking. You look at it closely and identify five mistakes. List the mistakes below.

SCHEDULE OF TEST RESULTS

Contractor	Address/location of dist board	Type of supply	Instruments	
Swayburn Electrics Ltd	Electrical supply room of the Hair and Beauty Salon, Staycation Hotel	3 phase		
Test date		Ze at origin	RCD tester	RCD TI 27
10th February		0.34 ohms	Continuity	CON TI 2
	Equipment vulnerable to testing	PFC	Insulation	IRT TI 5
Signature	Fibre optic and data cabling		Loop impedance	EFLP TI 1
Amir Hussein				

Description of Work

Circuit Description	Overcurrent device Short circuit capacity		Wiring conductors		Test results					Polarity	Earth loop imped-ance Zs	Functional testing		Remarks
	Type	Rating	Live mm²	CPC mm²	Continuity			Insulation resistance				RCD Time ms	Other	
					R1+R2	R2	Ring	Live / Live	Live / earth					
Ring final to manager's office	B	32	2.5	1.5	0.19	0.19	0.24	200MΩ	200MΩ	✓	0.24	N/A	N/A	
Ring final to reception	B	32	2.5	1.5	0.19	0.19	0.24	2Ω	200MΩ	✓	0.24	N/A	N/A	
Sauna	B	32	2.5	1.5	N/A	N/A	N/A	200MΩ	200MΩ	✓	0.25	N/A	N/A	
Lighting circuit to male changing room	B	6	1.5	2.5	N/A	N/A	N/A	200MΩ	200MΩ	✓	0.24	N/A	N/A	

Deviations from wiring regulations and special notes There are no unusual deviations in this installation

The errors are:

1.

2.

3.

4.

5.

Four of the errors are likely to be recording errors and attention to detail. However, one error indicates there is a fault on a circuit. This would require further investigation and re-testing. Highlight this error.

Your questions answered...

I often hear people refer to Guidance Note GS 38. What is it and is it important?

GS 38 is published by the Health and Safety Executive. It is for electrical testing equipment used by electricians. The document gives guidance to electrically competent people involved in electrical testing, diagnosis and repair. Electrically competent people may include electricians, electrical contractors, test supervisors, technicians, managers or appliance repairers. Advice is given on:

- test probes/leads
- voltage-indicating devices
- systems of work.

The probes:

- have finger barriers or are shaped to guard against inadvertent hand contact with the live conductors under test
- are insulated to leave an exposed metal tip not exceeding 4 mm measured across any surface of the tip. Where practicable, it is strongly recommended that this is reduced to 2 mm or less, or that spring-loaded retractable screened probes are used
- should have suitable high breaking capacity (HBC), sometimes known as HRC, fuse or fuses, with a low current rating (usually not exceeding 500 mA), or a current-limiting resistor and a fuse.

The leads:

- are adequately insulated (choice of insulating material may be influenced by the environment in which the leads are to be used)
- are coloured so that one lead can be easily distinguished from the other
- are flexible and of sufficient capacity for the duty expected of them
- are sheathed to protect against mechanical damage
- are long enough for the purpose, while not too long so that they are clumsy or unwieldy
- do not have accessible exposed conductors other than the probe tips, or have live conductors accessible to a person's finger if a lead becomes detached from a probe, indicator or instrument when in use. The test lead or leads are held captive and sealed into the body of the voltage detector.

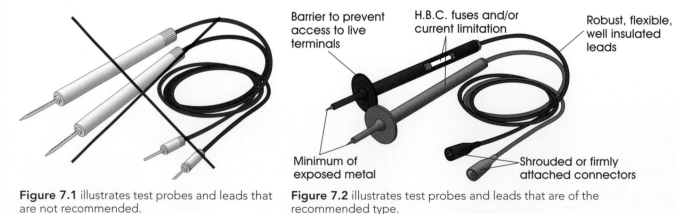

Figure 7.1 illustrates test probes and leads that are not recommended.

Figure 7.2 illustrates test probes and leads that are of the recommended type.

QUICK QUIZ

1. On the initial verification you check for damaged or defective cables.
   True/False

2. On inspection you check the protective device is the correct rating.
   True/False

3. On inspection you check to see there are no breaks in the ring circuit.
   True/False

4. The regulation covering leisure complexes states all electrical installations should be checked every five years.
   True/False

5. Extremely long lengths of cables reduce volt drop.
   True/False

UNIT 308

Understanding the principles, practices and legislation for diagnosing and correcting faults in electrotechnical systems and equipment in buildings, structures and the environment

Electricians are trained to a high standard to provide a competent, reliable and safe service to our customers. Electricians should not only be capable of installing wiring systems and equipment to a high standard, they should also have the ability to recognise when something is not up to standard or is not functioning correctly – for example, when a piece of equipment is not suitable or a circuit is not operating correctly. Unsuitable equipment could be a metal-clad switch in a damp environment. For this situation we must understand that the moisture would lead to the corrosion of the metal, thus reducing the integrity of the switch and making it unsafe to use! We could class the recognition of such a problem as a visual fault, which could be noted during a periodic inspection of an installation. In the case of a circuit not operating correctly, this could be a two-way lighting circuit only operating from one switch. This type of fault should be found before energising the circuit.

It is part of your training to gain such knowledge and understanding of wiring systems and equipment, which will lead to you becoming a competent electrician or even a future designer.

You need to be aware that not all faults are easily visible; some are concealed and may develop over a period of time. Such faults can be limited by regular testing and inspection.

Testing is not only needed at the completion of works, but should also take place during the installation process of the wiring system.

Regular inspection, tests and maintenance checks should be used over periods of time to confirm quality and extend the life of the electrical installation.

You will need to understand the following:
➤ the principles, regulatory requirements and procedures for completing the safe isolation of electrical circuits and complete installations
➤ how to complete the reporting and recording of electrical fault diagnosis and correction work
➤ how to complete the preparatory work for fault diagnosis and correction work
➤ the procedures and techniques for diagnosing electrical faults
➤ the procedures and techniques for correcting electrical faults

Key knowledge

➤ Safe isolation

➤ How to diagnose electrical faults

➤ How to correct electrical faults

➤ How to report and record electrical faults

Project scenario

This scenario continues from the Staycation Hotel development project first introduced in Unit 303. You may need to refer back to this unit to remind yourself of the key personnel and the work scenario.

Preparatory work for fault diagnosis

ACTIVITY

The day for the hotel opening party is fast approaching, and Swayburn Electrics are on schedule to complete all the work in both parts of the hotel on time.

As part of the pre-commissioning inspection **test**, Amir recorded a reading of only 2Ω on the ring final to the reception. You initially re-test the ring final to see if it was simply a recording error on the paperwork, but the test result comes back again as 2Ω. This confirms there is a problem in the ring circuit. List and describe the possible causes of this low reading. You should be able to identify at least five possible causes.

1.

2.

3.

4.

5.

ACTIVITY

The list below contains the essential stages for logical fault-finding and fault diagnosis. The list is not in the correct order. Number the stages in the correct order and outline what each stage entails.

Ordered stages for logical fault finding	Number in sequence	Description for each stage
Isolation and test		
Carry out functional tests		
Interpret information and test results		
Identify the symptom		
Restore the supply		
Gather information		
Check protective devices		
Analyse the evidence		
Rectify the fault		
Check supply		

Figure 8.1: Some common electrical faults: overloading by installing too many cables into a connector block.

ACTIVITY

Having completed the series of fault-finding stages, you discover the cause to be a pinched cable in the back of one of the sockets. This was due to poor installation work by Robert, who is still on his probation period. You are in a bit of a dilemma – there is already friction between you and Robert as he perceives himself to be older and more experienced than you. However, the poor workmanship, if left unchecked, could lead to potential risks for the client or a danger to the public.

1. Who should you report the fault to?

2. Should you inform the site manager?

3. How would you inform Robert about the fault?

4. Would you inform James Swayburn about this incident?

5. Who do you think should make good the fault?

ACTIVITY

1. What are the legal requirements for providing a safe fire evacuation procedure in your workplace?

2. How does COSHH affect your planning before your team starts work on an electrical installation?

Figure 8.2: Some common electrical faults: damage to a cable from a screw.

Costing and fault repairs

ACTIVITY

The hotel opens on time and the launch event is a great success. Two weeks later, you receive a call from Chardonnay, complaining that the lights have stopped working in the cutting and styling area and the washing machine in the laundry room works intermittently. They know there isn't a fault with the actual washing machine as they have called out a service engineer, and he reports that it is a problem with the supply. Chardonnay says the faults have to be fixed *immediately* as they are losing business because the hairdressers cannot cut hair in poor lighting. Also, with the washing machine being temperamental, Chardonnay and other members of staff have been taking the salon towels home to wash.

You are currently working on a new housing development which has proved to be a very demanding job. Robert no longer works for Swayburn Electrics – he decided he preferred being self-employed and has set up as a contractor. Amir is currently on a two-week block release at the local college, finishing his Technical Certificate.

Listed in the table below are some factors that need to be taken into consideration when **diagnosing** and rectifying the faults that have been reported. You need to consider all the factors below before speaking to James to get authorisation to complete the work.

	Implications for you and Swayburn Electrics Ltd	Implications for the hair and beauty salon
Costs of diagnosing and repairing the fault		
Availability of staff		
Availability of replacement resources		
Downtime		
Legal and personal responsibility		
Access to the salon (timing)		
Provision of emergency lighting		

Figure 8.3: Some common electrical faults: cable burnt out due to overloading of the circuit.

key terms

Diagnosis the analysis of problems within a faulty wiring system and the associated investigation.

ACTIVITY

You have reported this incident to James and asked him for authorisation to leave your current site to undertake the fault-finding at the hair and beauty salon. James is unhappy, but as Staycation Hotels are an important client with the potential for additional work on their forthcoming new builds, he has said you should respond to Chardonnay as soon as possible.

However, he doesn't want this issue to have a negative impact on your work on the current housing development site.

From the list below, identify which test instruments and equipment you think you would need to take with you and explain why.

Test equipment	What would this be used to test for?	Would you require this test instrument for the faults indicated in the salon? Why?
Voltage indicator		
Low resistance ohm meter		
Insulation resistance testers		
EFLI and PFC tester		
RCD tester		
Tong tester/clamp-on ammeter		
Phase sequence tester		

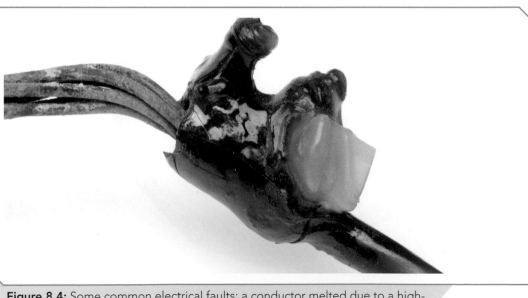

Figure 8.4: Some common electrical faults: a conductor melted due to a high-resistance termintation.

Your questions answered...

I often hear the phrase 'transient voltages'. What are they and how do they create faults?

A transient voltage can be defined as a variance or disturbance to the normal voltage level.

This type of fault is becoming increasingly problematic with the expanding use of IT equipment, not only in commerce and industry, but also in the home.

The normal voltage level is the voltage band in which the equipment is designed to operate. It is the installation designer's responsibility to stipulate adequate conductor sizes for the circuits installed. This sizing procedure will only prevent voltage drop during normal circuit condition.

The designer cannot prevent transient voltages as they are outside of their control, but he can compensate by including equipment that protects against such voltage variations and disturbances. It is now becoming common practice to install filter systems to IT circuits, which provide stabilised voltage levels. These devices can also reduce the effect of voltage spikes by suppressing them.

If transient voltages are not recognised, they can cause damage to equipment and lead to a loss of data, which could prove costly to many consumers such as banks and industry, as they rely on data movement and storage.

If this type of fault is thought to exist on installations, monitoring equipment can be installed to record events over periods of time. The results of the monitoring can usually trace the cause of transient voltages.

Common causes of transient voltages are:
- supply company faults
- electronic equipment
- heavy current switching (causing voltage drops)
- earth fault voltages
- lightning strikes.

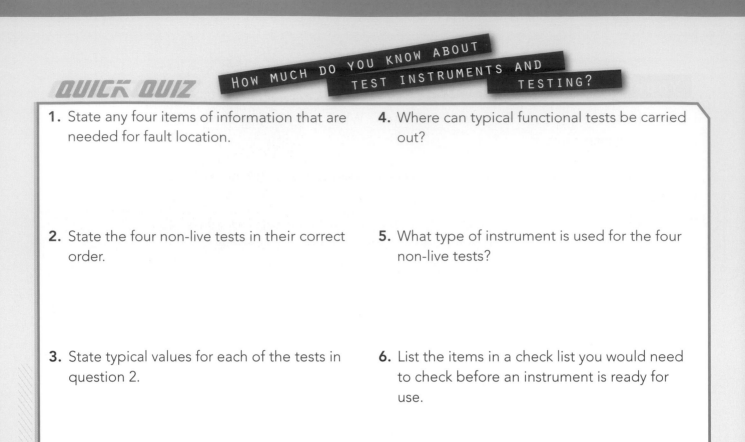

1. State any four items of information that are needed for fault location.

2. State the four non-live tests in their correct order.

3. State typical values for each of the tests in question 2.

4. Where can typical functional tests be carried out?

5. What type of instrument is used for the four non-live tests?

6. List the items in a check list you would need to check before an instrument is ready for use.

UNIT 309

Understanding the electrical principles associated with the design, building, installation and maintenance of electrical equipment and systems

The jobs a competent electrician will have to carry out are many and varied. However, as well as having the ability to practically carry out these jobs – such as installing a motor – electricians also need to know about the operating principles of that piece of equipment so it can be installed correctly. This unit looks at the principles of electrical science necessary to support the electrician so a full understanding of the scientific principles is developed.

You will need to understand the following:
- ➤ mathematical principles appropriate to electrical installations and design work
- ➤ standard units of measurement used in electrical installation, maintenance and design work
- ➤ basic mechanics and the relationship between force, work, energy and power
- ➤ the relationship between resistance, resistivity, voltage, current and power
- ➤ the fundamental principles which underpin the relationship between magnetism and electricity
- ➤ electrical supply and distribution systems
- ➤ how different electrical properties can affect electrical circuits, systems and equipment
- ➤ the operating principles and applications of DC machines and AC motors
- ➤ the operating principles of different electrical components
- ➤ the principles and applications of electrical lighting systems
- ➤ the principles and applications of electrical heating
- ➤ the types, applications and limitations of electronic components in electrotechnical systems and equipment

Key knowledge

➤ SI units

➤ Fractions

➤ Algebra

➤ Indices

➤ Transposition

➤ Trigonometry

➤ Statistics

➤ Mechanics

➤ Electron theory

➤ Series and parallel DC circuits

➤ Magnetism and electricity

➤ Inductance, reactance and capacitance

➤ Power factor

➤ Supply and distribution

➤ Star and delta connections

➤ Transformers

➤ DC machines

➤ Controlling motors

➤ Illumination

➤ Water heating

➤ Electronics

Standard units of measurement

SI units

When engineers, scientists and technicians get together to work on design and construction projects, they need to use a common language or form of expression to understand each other. Before we are able to communicate in an electrical sense, we must first understand the units we will all use and the ways in which we will use those units in a mathematical manner.

In the United Kingdom and many other European countries, an international system of units is used which are known as the Système Internationale (SI) units.

Each of these units has a symbol to represent it, but these should not be confused with the unit names. These will become more apparent and make more sense as they are used in different formulae and equations.

ACTIVITY

The following two tables list the SI units you need to be able to recognise and identify. Complete the table, putting in the correct symbol, name and definition of the quantity in your own words.

Quantity	Symbol	Name	Definition
Length	*m*	*Metre*	*The linear extent from one end to the other*
Area			
Volume			
Mass			
Density			
Time			
Temperature			
Velocity			

ACTIVITY

Working in small groups, complete the table. Agree among yourselves on the correct symbol and write a description of where this quantity can be found and used in electrical installation work.

Quantity	Symbol	Description of where this quantity can be found
Resistance	Ω	*A material's opposition to the flow of electric current; measured in ohms. Often used in reference to electrical cables.*
Resistivity		
Power		
Frequency		
Current		
Voltage		
Energy		
Impedance		
Inductance and inductive reactance		
Capacitance and capacitive reactance		
Power factor		
Actual power		
Reactive power		
Apparent power		

Mathematical principles

Fractions

Fractions are really just a means of expressing how many bits of a whole number we have left if we break it up (or divide it) by another number.

However, there is another way to think about this.

For example, consider the following:

$$1 \div 8 = \frac{1}{8}$$

Or, in other words, if I have one block of electrical connectors and break it into eight equal parts, then take seven of them away, it could be said that I am left with one part out of the original eight, or one out of a possible eight.

Expressed as a fraction, this would be: $\frac{1}{8}$ (one out of eight available).

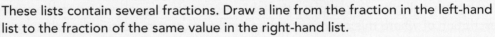

ACTIVITY

These lists contain several fractions. Draw a line from the fraction in the left-hand list to the fraction of the same value in the right-hand list.

$\frac{3}{5}$		$\frac{3}{10}$
$\frac{2}{3}$		$\frac{5}{12}$
$\frac{1}{4}$		$\frac{8}{36}$
$\frac{3}{24}$		$\frac{25}{30}$
$\frac{6}{21}$		$\frac{1}{2}$
$\frac{4}{44}$		$\frac{12}{20}$
$\frac{3}{5}$		$\frac{8}{12}$
$\frac{9}{30}$		$\frac{2}{7}$
$\frac{6}{12}$		$\frac{1}{11}$
$\frac{5}{6}$		$\frac{1}{8}$
$\frac{2}{9}$		$\frac{9}{15}$
$\frac{20}{48}$		$\frac{5}{20}$

Algebra

Algebra is probably the area of mathematics that causes the most problems.

However, without a good understanding of these areas, you will find it almost impossible to pass the examinations and become a qualified electrician.

Algebra is nothing more than a means of solving maths problems. But instead of using numbers, we use letters or symbols to represent unknown quantities

'In algebra, we normally miss out the multiplication sign.'

As an example, if we were given	$(ab)c$
This is effectively saying	$(a \times b) \times c$

'It doesn't matter which letter comes first.'

So, if we were given the sum	$a + b$
it also means	$b + a$

This is exactly the same as if you were adding 4 to 3 or 3 to 4; both equal 7.

'There is more than one way to write the same thing.'

If we were given the sum	$a(b + c)$
Then we could also say	$a \times (b + c)$
And we could also say	$(a \times b) + (a \times c)$

All of the above statements are true.

Here is another example:

$$\frac{a + b}{c}$$

In this one, the letters a and b are both going to be divided by c.

We could re-write this as:

$$\frac{a}{c} + \frac{b}{c}$$

'If you want to check your answer, put some simple numbers in.'

If you have the question $x = y + z$, where $x = 12$, $y = 8$, and $z = 4$, then put the numbers in to see if you are correct: $12 = 8 + 4$

ACTIVITY

Solving the equations below.

Worked example

Find the answer for the equation	$12ge - 3ek + ekg$
where	$g = 1, e = 3$ and $k = 5$

We should now re-write the equation to include the mathematics symbols:

First, the brackets:	$12(ge) - 3(ek) + (egk)$
Second, the various signs:	$12 \times (g \times e) - 3 \times (e \times k) + (g \times e \times k)$

Now replace the letters with the numbers you were given:

	$12 \times (1 \times 3) - 3 \times (3 \times 5) + (1 \times 3 \times 5)$
Multiply inside the brackets:	$12 \times (3) - 3 \times (15) + (15)$
This gives you:	$36 - 45 + 15$
Answer:	6

1. Find the answer for the equation $10bn - 3bj + bnj$
   when $b = 1$; $n = 3$; and $j = 5$

2. Find the answer for the equation $8cd + 3cdf + 2f$
   when $c = 1$, $d = 3$ and $f = 5$

3. Find the answer for the equation $4xy + 3xyz - 2yz$
   when $x = 1$, $y = 3$ and $z = 4$

Indices

Indices are best explained by an example.

If we multiply two identical numbers (say, 4 and 4) and the answer is 16, the process is usually expressed as:

$$4 \times 4 = 16$$

However, we could express the same calculation as $4^2 = 16$.

The raised 2 simply means that the 4 is multiplied by itself. The raised 2 is known as the index. Sometimes this is referred to as 'four raised to the power of two'.

Therefore, 4^3 means four multiplied by itself three time: $4 \times 4 \times 4 = 64$.

Do not make the mistake of thinking that $4^3 = 4 \times 3$.

Here are some examples of indices:

$$2^3 = 2 \times 2 \times 2 = 8$$
$$9^3 = 9 \times 9 \times 9 = 729$$
$$6^2 = 6 \times 6 = 36$$

A number by itself (say, 7), has an invisible index (^{1}), but this is not normally shown.

Consider 7×7^2

This could be shown as $7 \times 7 \times 7$ or as 7^3, which would mean that the indices ^{2} and (the invisible) ^{1} have been added together.

The rule is, when multiplying, add the indices.

Examples

$8 \times 8^2 = 8^1 \times 8^2 = 8^3 = 8 \times 8 \times 8 = 512$

$5 \times 5^3 \times 5^2 = 5^1 \times 5^3 \times 5^2 = 5^6 = 5 \times 5 \times 5 \times 5 \times 5 \times 5 = 15{,}625$

Let's move on to the following situation:

$$5^3 \times \frac{1}{5^2} \text{ is the same as } \frac{5^3}{5^2} = \frac{5 \times 5 \times 5}{5 \times 5}$$

Cancelling out the fives $\dfrac{\cancel{5} \times \cancel{5} \times 5}{\cancel{5} \times \cancel{5}}$ gives us the answer: 5

This means that the indices have been subtracted: $3 - 2$

The rule is, when dividing, subtract the indices.

How about this: $4 - 2$ is either: 4 subtract 2; or 4 add -2.

Remember, the addition of indices goes with multiplication.

So from this we can see that 5^4 divided by 5^2 is the same as 5^4 multiplied by 5^{-2}. Therefore:

$$\frac{1}{5^2} \text{ is the same as } 5^{-2}$$

Further examples of this are:

$$\frac{1}{4^3} = 4^{-3} \qquad \frac{1}{2^6} = 2^{-6}$$

We can now see that indices can be moved above or below the line, providing the sign is changed.

Some further examples:

$$\frac{5^6 \times 5^7 \times 5^{-3}}{5^4 \times 5^2} \qquad = \frac{5^{13} \times 5^3}{5^6} \qquad = \frac{5^{10}}{5^6}$$

$$= 5^{10} \times 5^{-6} \qquad = 5^4 \qquad = 5 \times 5 \times 5 \times 5 = 625$$

And finally:

$$(5^4 \times 5^{-6}) \times (5^{-4} \times 5^3) = (5^4 \times 5^{-6}) \times (5^{-1}) \times 5^4 \times 5^{-6} \times 5^{-1} = 5^4 \times 5^{-7}$$

$$= 5^{-3} \qquad = \frac{1}{5^3} \qquad = \frac{1}{125} = 0.008$$

ACTIVITY

Calculate the following indices:

1. $9 \times 9^3 \times 9^2$

2. $3 \times 3^3 \times 3^7$

3. $\dfrac{6 \times 6^7 \times 6^{-3}}{6^4 \times 6^2}$

4. $\dfrac{5^7 \times 5^{-3}}{5^4 \times 5^2}$

Transposition

Transposition is a method using principles of mathematics, which will allow you to rearrange a formula or equation so you can find an unknown quantity.

However, there is one important rule that must always be followed – without fail!

What you do to one side of the equation, you must do to the other side

Let's look some examples.

Example 1

Transpose this formula (re-arrange it) to make G the subject (the one we want):

$G = T + Z$

First, think of transposition as being a pair of scales, and remember that each side of the scales (each side of the equals sign) must be balanced. Second, when we want to remove something, we perform an opposite operation.

To get T by itself, we must remove Z.

But, as Z has been added to T, we need to perform 'an opposite operation'. In other words we need to *subtract* Z from both sides of the equation to keep it balanced.

To do this: $G = T + Z$ becomes $\quad G - \mathbf{Z} = T + Z - \mathbf{Z}$

As $+ Z - \mathbf{Z}$ cancels itself out, you're left with $G - Z = T$

Example 2

Transpose $B = Q - LS$ so Q is the subject of the equation.

To get Q by itself, we need to get rid of LS.

This is currently being subtracted from Q, so we need to *add* it to both sides:

$$B + \mathbf{LS} = Q - LS + \mathbf{LS}$$

Remember that $- LS + \mathbf{LS}$ cancels out.

This means that when we complete the calculation we have an answer of $B + LS = Q$

However, we can view multiplication and division in much the same way.

Transpose the formula $V = I \times R$ to make I the subject.

If we follow through with our idea of opposite operations, we can see that at the moment I has been multiplied by R.

Therefore, to leave I by itself, we must divide by R on both sides.

$$V = I \times R \text{ becomes } \frac{V}{\mathbf{R}} = \frac{I \times R}{\mathbf{R}}$$

If you carry out this calculation you're left with an answer of $\frac{V}{R} = I$

Resistivity example

This equation describes how resistance is related to length, area and type of material.

$$R = \frac{\rho L}{A}$$

Transpose this equation to find L.

First, we need to get rid of A. As it is currently dividing into ρL, we need to multiply both sides by A.

Therefore:

$$R = \frac{\rho L}{A} \text{ becomes } R \times A = \frac{\rho L \times A}{A},$$

giving us $R \times A = \rho L$.

We need to get rid of ρ.

This is currently multiplying L, so we must divide by ρ on both sides.

Therefore: $R \times A = \rho L$ becomes

$$\frac{R \times A}{\rho} = \frac{\rho L}{\rho}, \text{ giving us } R \times A = \frac{L}{\rho}$$

George Simon Ohm, a German physicist discovered that, at a constant temperature, the current flowing in a circuit is directly proportional to the voltage. So the voltage (V) is equal to the current (I) × resistance (R). Therefore Ohm's law can be expressed by the following formula.

$$V = I \times R$$

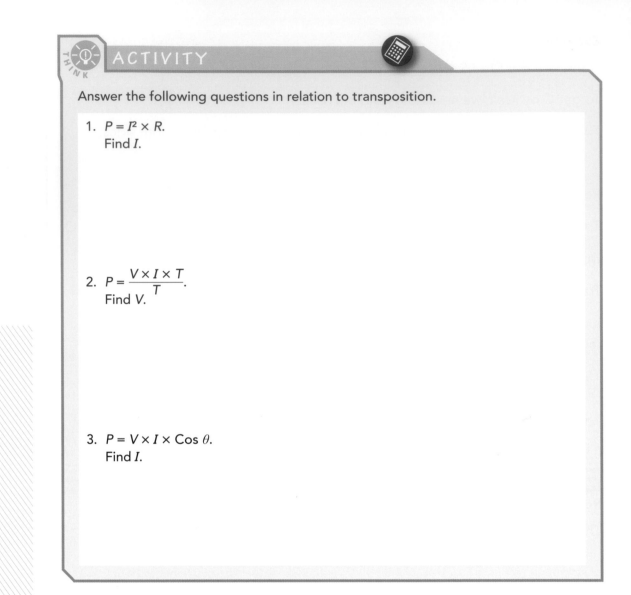

ACTIVITY

Answer the following questions in relation to transposition.

1. $P = I^2 \times R$.
    Find I.

2. $P = \dfrac{V \times I \times T}{T}$.
    Find V.

3. $P = V \times I \times \text{Cos } \theta$.
    Find I.

Triangles and trigonometry

Pythagoras' theorem states that for a right-angled triangle, the square of the *hypotenuse* is equal to the sum of the squares on the two adjacent sides.

In simple terms, this means that if you know the length of two of the sides, you can find out the length of the third.

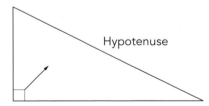

Hypotenuse

We can see that the right angle (often represented as a square in the corner of the triangle) is like an arrow head, and it always points at the longest side, which is the hypotenuse.

For ease, lets call the hypotenuse side (*a*) and the other two sides (*b*) and (*c*).

The Pythagoras formula is $a^2 = b^2 + c^2$

key terms

Pythagoras' theorem
formula for calculating the length of sides in right-angled triangles. Named after Pythagoras, an ancient Greek mathematician.

For example, if you know that one side wall is 30 metres high and the other is 40 metres long, then you use Pythagoras' theorem to work out the diagonal (hypotenuse).

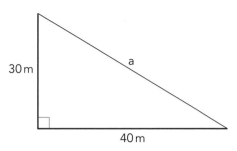

Using the formula $a^2 = b^2 + c^2$

$a^2 = 30^2 + 40^2$

$a^2 = 900 + 1,600$ = $a^2 = 2,500$

$\therefore a = 50\,m$

Trigonometry

Trigonometry is all about the relationship between the angles and sides of triangles.

We have just discovered that in a right-angled triangle, we call the long side the hypotenuse and the right angle 'points' at it. The side of the triangle opposite to the angle being considered is called the *opposite* and the side next to the angle under consideration and the right angle, is called the *adjacent*.

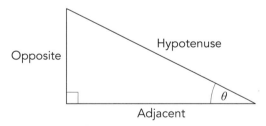

In the above drawing, (θ) is the angle to be considered.

We already know that the longest side is the hypotenuse, so the one that's left must be the adjacent.

The next step relates to the: *tangent, sine* and *cosine*.

These are used to show the ratio between angles and sides. You choose which one you need depending on the information you have been given.

Consequently:

$$\textbf{S}ine\ \theta = \frac{\text{Opposite}}{\text{Hypotenuse}} \qquad \textbf{C}osine\ \theta = \frac{\text{Adjacent}}{\text{Hypotenuse}} \qquad \textbf{T}angent\ \theta = \frac{\text{Opposite}}{\text{Adjacent}}$$

To help you remember them, try to remember SOH CAH TOA. It's the letters highlighted in each formula (for example, SOH – sine is equal to opposite over hypotenuse).

Examples find the value of angle (θ)

In this example we are given details about the opposite and adjacent sides, so we'll use the tangent formula. The shaded area indicates a typical calculator function for use with these calculations. Ensure you have a calculator with these functions. If you are unsure, ask your class tutor.

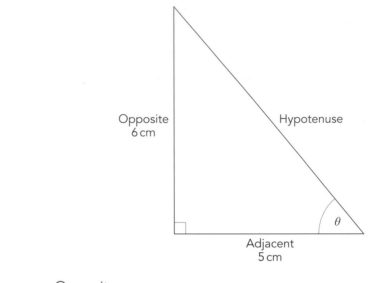

$$\text{Tangent } \theta = \frac{\text{Opposite}}{\text{Adjacent}}$$

$$\text{Tangent } \theta = \frac{6}{5} = 12$$

Find the angle that has a tan of 1.2. Entering 1.2 into your calculator, then press the INV key and then the TAN key. The answer should be 50.19°.

ACTIVITY

THINK

1. Find the value of angle (θ).

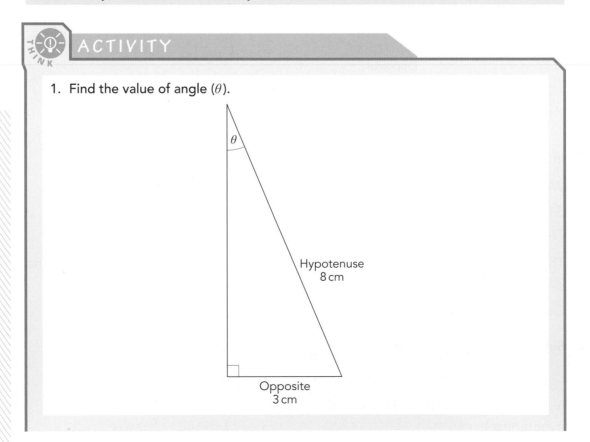

2. Find the value of angle (θ).
   This time we have information about the adjacent and hypotenuse, so we use the cosine formula.

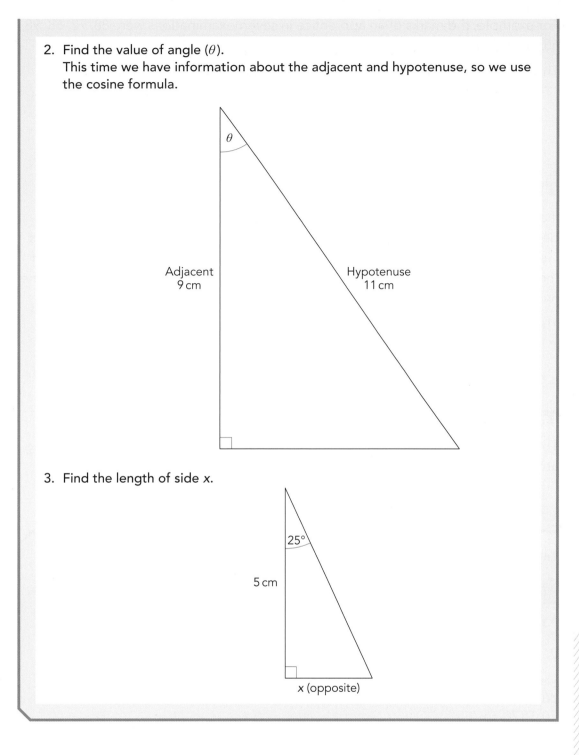

3. Find the length of side *x*.

Statistics

There are many ways to record and display data. In statistics the following kinds of average are used.

The mean

The mean is the commonest type of average. It is determined by adding all of the items in the set and dividing the result by the number of items.

Mean = the total of all the items divided by the number of items

For example, the marks of an apprentice in seven examinations were 88, 72, 68, 98, 65, 68 and 77.

The mean of his marks is:

$$88 + 72 + 68 + 98 + 65 + 68 + 66 \div 7$$

$$= 525 \div 7$$

$$= 75$$

The median

If a distribution is arranged so that all the items are arranged in ascending (or descending) order of size, the median is the value that is half way along the series. Generally there will be an equal number of items below and above the median. If there is an even number of items, the median is found by taking the average of the two middle items.

The median of the range:

65, 66, 68, 68, 72, 88, 98

is 68

The mode

The value that occurs most frequently in a distribution is called the mode. Looking at the example above, 68 occurs most often, so 68 is the mode.

ACTIVITY

Complete the table, filling in the values for mode, mean and median.

Values	Mean	Median	Mode
The ages of students in your class are: 16, 16, 16, 16, 16, 17, 17, 17, 18, 18, 18, 18, 18, 19, 19, 23, 23, 27			
The hourly pay your colleagues get is: £5.50, £5.50, £5.50, £5.60, £5.60, £5.70, £5.70, £5.70, £5.70, £5.70, £5.70, £5.80, £5.90, £5.80, £5.90, £5.80, £5.90, £5.80, £5.90			
The number of hours your colleagues work per week are: 30hrs, 30hrs, 30hrs, 30hrs, 30hrs, 30hrs, 31hrs, 32hrs, 35hrs, 31hrs, 32hrs, 35hrs, 31hrs, 32hrs, 35hrs, 37hrs, 38hrs, 40hrs, 40hrs, 40hrs, 40hrs			
The results you received in your exams are: 55%, 55%, 56%, 56%, 57%, 57%, 57%, 57%, 67%, 67%, 68%, 69%, 70%, 75%, 77%, 78%, 80%, 88%, 88%, 89%			

Basic mechanics

Mechanics is a way humans have devised to make and use machines to make life easier to work in.

A simple machine could be defined as a device that helps us perform our work more easily when a force is applied to it.

A screw, wheel and axle and lever are all simple machines. To make any simple machine work for us, we need to apply a force to it.

It also allows us to use a smaller force to overcome a larger force and can also help us change the direction of the force and work at a greater speed.

ACTIVITY

Levers, gears and pulleys are all types of 'machine' developed to make life easier for working. Find examples of these machines and draw diagrams of them in the space provided below. Write in your own words how these machines work.

1. Levers

2. Gears

3. Pulleys

Electrical energy

The basic unit of work or energy is the joule (J), but this is a very small unit and only represents a power of one watt for one second. To avoid silly calculations (imagine if we measured our working day in seconds, not hours), we therefore must use a much larger unit.

The unit used for electrical energy is the kilowatt-hour, which represents one kilowatt for one hour. From this we can see that:

1 joule (J) = 1 watt (W) for one second (s)

1,000 J = 1 kilowatt (kW) for one second

In one hour there are 3,600 seconds. Therefore

3,600 s × 1,000 J = 1 kW for one hour (kWh)

The kilowatt-hour is the unit used by electrical supply companies to charge their customers for the supply of electrical energy.

ACTIVITY

When you get home tonight after college, have a look in your house. Check the distribution unit and the electricity meter.

You'll see that the electric meter measures in kWh. However, these are more often referred to as units by the time they appear on your bill!

Efficiency

Can you perform every task given, to the best of your ability and 100 per cent efficiently, all of the time?

Most people and machines struggle to do this, because there are always 'things' that get in our way and try to slow us down. Think of a motor trying to run. It has to continually overcome the friction of the bearings it turns on.

Consequently, the ratio of the effort that we have to put in, against the product coming out the other end, is known as **efficiency**.

We can show efficiency with the formula:

$$\text{Percentage efficiency} = \frac{\text{Output}}{\text{Inut}} \times 100$$

For example: calculate the efficiency of a water heater if the output is 25 kWh and the input energy is 30 kWh.

$$\text{Efficiency (\%)} = \frac{\text{Output}}{\text{Input}} \times 100$$

$$= \frac{25}{30} \times 100$$

$$= 83.33\%$$

key terms

Efficiency the efficiency of a system is the ratio of the output to the input .

ACTIVITY

1. The power output from a generator is 2,700 W and the power required to drive it is 3,500 W. Calculate the percentage efficiency of the generator.

Resistance, voltage, current and power

Every substance is composed of **molecules**, which in turn are made up of atoms. Molecules are always in a state of rapid motion, but when they are densely packed together, this movement is restricted and the substance formed by these molecules is solid.

When the molecules of a substance are less tightly bound, there is a great deal of free movement. Such a substance is known as a liquid. When the molecule movement is almost unrestricted, the substance can expand and contract in any direction – this known as a gas.

However, atoms themselves are not solid, but consist of even smaller particles. At the centre of each atom is the **nucleus**, which is made up from particles, known as **protons** and protons are said to possess a positive charge.

The remaining particles in an atom are known as **electrons**. These orbit around the nucleus and are said to possess a negative charge.

All atoms possess equal numbers of protons and electrons. Thus, the positive and negative charges are cancelled out, leaving the atom electrically neutral.

Perhaps the simplest explanation is to look to our solar system, where we have a central star, the sun, around which are the orbiting planets. In the tiny atom the protons form a central nucleus (the sun) and the electrons are the orbiting particles (planets)

The simplest atom is hydrogen, which has one proton and one electron. The diagram shows the hydrogen atom.

Electrons are arranged in layers at varying distances from the nucleus – those nearest the nucleus are more strongly held in place than those farthest away. These distant electrons are easily moved from their orbits and so are free to join those of another atom, whose own distant electrons may in turn leave to join another atom, and so on.

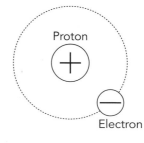

Proton

Electron

It is these wandering (or 'free') electrons moving about the molecular structure of a material that we know as electricity.

We call a material that allows the movement of free electrons a **conductor**, while one that doesn't is an **insulator**.

key terms

Molecule a group of atoms bonded together.

Nucleus the positively charged central core of an atom made up of protons – has a positive charge.

Proton a stable subatomic particle occurring in all atoms – has a positive charge.

Electron a stable subatomic particle with a negative charge.

key terms

Conductor a material that conducts electricity.

Insulator a material that doesn't readily conduct electricity.

ACTIVITY

Complete the table, listing as many items as you can that are insulators and conductors used in the electrical industry. Describe how and why they are used in the industry. You can ask colleagues and use the internet.

Insulator	Why used (good points)	How used
Rubber		
Plastic		
Magnesium oxide		
Mica		
Porcelain		
Rigid plastics		
Wood		
Glass		

Conductor	Why used (good points)	How used
Aluminium		
Brass		
Copper		
Carbon		
Iron/steel		
Lead		
Mercury		
Tungsten		
Sodium		
Gold		

Series and parallel DC circuits

Series circuits

If a number of resistors are connected together end-to-end and then connected to a battery, the current can only take one route through the circuit. This type of connection is called a series circuit.

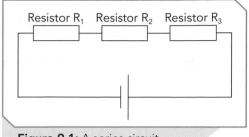

Figure 9.1: A series circuit.

The following rules apply to a series circuit:

➤ The total circuit resistance (R_t) is equal to the sum of all the circuit resistors. In other words, to find the total resistance of the circuit, we add up the value of the individual resistors. In our diagram, this would be: $R_t = R_1 + R_2 + R_3$.

➤ The total circuit current (I) is equal to the battery **emf** divided by the total resistance. This is just Ohm's law again. Remember: $I = V/R$.

➤ The current will have the same value at any point in the circuit.

➤ The potential difference across each resistor is proportional to its resistance.

key terms

Emf the electromotive force or the force that causes the flow of electrons.

If we think back to Ohm's law, we use voltage to push the electrons through a resistor. How much we use depends on the size of the resistor. The bigger the resistor, the more we use.

Therefore: $V_1 = I \times R_1$; $V_2 = I \times R_2$; etc.

The supply voltage (V) will be equal to the sum of the potential differences across each resistor. In other words, if we add up the p.d. across each resistor (the amount of volts 'dropped' across each resistor), it should come to the value of the supply voltage.

We show this as: $V = V_1 + V_2 + V_3$

The total power in a series circuit is equal to the sum of the individual powers used by each resistor. In other words, $P = P_1 + P_2 + P_3$

Parallel circuits

If a number of resistors are connected together as shown in Figure 9.2, they are said to be connected in parallel.

In this type of connection, the total current splits up and divides itself among the different branches of the circuit. However, it should be noted that the pressure pushing the electrons along (voltage), will be the same through each of the branches. Therefore, any branch of a parallel circuit can be disconnected without affecting the other remaining branches.

In summary, we can therefore say that the following rules will apply to a parallel circuit:

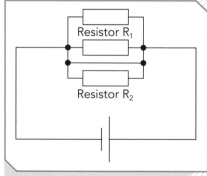

Figure 9.2: A parallel circuit.

➤ The total circuit current (I), is found by adding together the current through each of the branches: $I = I_1 + I_2 + I_3$.

➤ The same potential difference will occur across each branch of the circuit.

➤ $V = V_1 = V_2 = V_3$

Where resistors are connected in parallel, and for the purpose of calculation, it is easier if the group of resistors is replaced by one large resistor (R_t).

$$\frac{1}{R_t} = \frac{1}{R_1} = \frac{1}{R_2} = \frac{1}{R_3}$$

ACTIVITY

Answer the following questions related to series and parallel circuits.

1. An electric fire of resistance 24.8 Ω, an immersion heater of resistance 34.8 Ω, a small microwave oven of resistance 45.9 Ω and a toaster of resistance 120 Ω are connected to a 230 V power circuit. Calculate the current taken by each appliance and the total current drawn from the supply.

2. A 230 V electric kettle has a resistance of 88 Ω and is connected to a socket outlet by a twin cable, each conductor of which has a resistance of 0.1 Ω. The total resistance of the cable from fuse board to the socket is 0.8 Ω. Calculate the total resistance of the whole circuit.

3. Calculate the resistance and the current drawn from the supply by the following equipment connected to a 230 V supply:
   - a 4 kW 230 V immersion heater

   - a 600 W 230 V microwave oven

   - a 1 kW 230 V electric fire

   - a 750 W 230 V stereo system.

Magnetism and electricity

Whenever a conductor cuts the lines of a magnetic flux, an electromotive force (emf) is induced in that conductor.

The magnitude of the emf will be determined by:

➤ the *strength* of the magnetic field

➤ the *length* of the conductor cutting the lines of the magnetic flux

➤ the *speed* at which the conductor cuts the lines of magnetic flux

➤ the *angle* at which the conductor cuts the lines of magnetic flux.

ACTIVITY

1. Draw a diagram to illustrate Flemings *right-hand rule*.

Single-loop generator

ACTIVITY

This is a diagram of a single-loop generator. Using the diagram as a guide, describe the principle of how the generator works and describe what happens when the loop turns through one complete revolution.

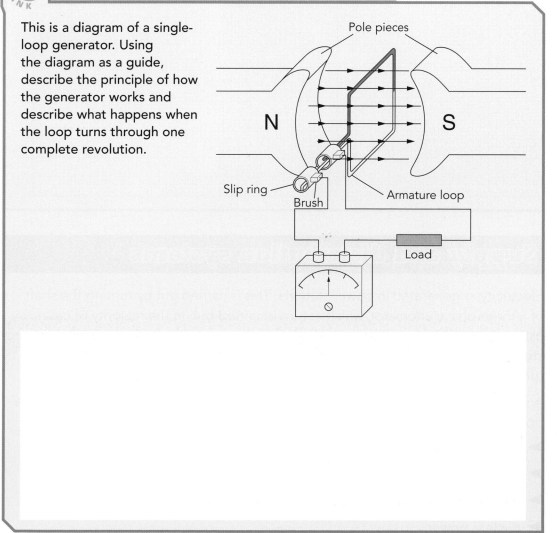

ACTIVITY

This is a diagram of a loop of wire connected to slip rings. When the loop starts to rotate, this conductor is moving parallel to the magnetic field, does not cut them, and therefore the induced emf is zero.

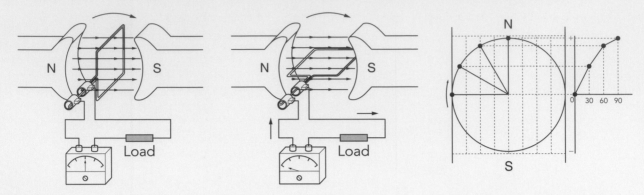

As the loop rotates from 0° to 90°, it cuts more and more lines of flux and at varying angles. As a result, the magnitude of the emf will vary up to the maximum when the loop is cutting lines of magnetic flux at right angles.

Plot a sine wave illustrating how the sine wave is developed as the loop moves through the magnetic field.

Supply and distribution systems

Electricity in generated in power stations. This is carried out by turning the shaft of a three-phase alternator, which in turn is carried out, in the majority of cases, by using steam. This steam is created by heating water until it becomes high-pressure steam. The steam is then forced onto the vanes of the steam turbine, which now turns the alternator.

A variety of energy sources are used to heat the water in the first place. The more popular ones are:

➤ coal

➤ gas

➤ oil

➤ nuclear power.

ACTIVITY

Draw a diagram of the basic components of a supply and distribution system. The diagram should include a heat-generating energy system, turbine, alternator, supply and distribution system.

Also label on the supply and distribution system the different voltages you may expect to find.

ACTIVITY

Complete the table, briefly describing how electricity can be generated from the listed energy sources.

Source of energy	Description of the main characteristics of how electricity is generated
Batteries and cells	
Solar power thermal	
Solar power photovoltaic	
Wind energy	
Wave energy	
Micro hydro	
Ground source heat pumps	
Combined heat and power	

Distribution to the customer

Once the electricity has left the local substation, it will eventually arrive at the customer.

Obviously there will be many different sizes of installation, but generally speaking we will find certain items at every main intake position. These items, which belong to the supply company, are:

➤ A sealed over current device that protects the supply company's cable.

➤ An energy metering system to determine the customer's electricity usage.

It is after this point that we say we have reached the consumer's installation.

The consumer's installation must be controlled by a main switch, which must be located as close as possible to the supply company equipment and be capable of isolating all phase conductors.

In the average domestic installation, this device is merged with the means of distributing and protecting the final circuits in what we know as the **consumer unit**.

Figure 9.3 shows the arrival of a 230V TN–S supply into a domestic property:

key terms

Consumer unit is a box of fuses or circuit breakers, usually arranged in a single row.

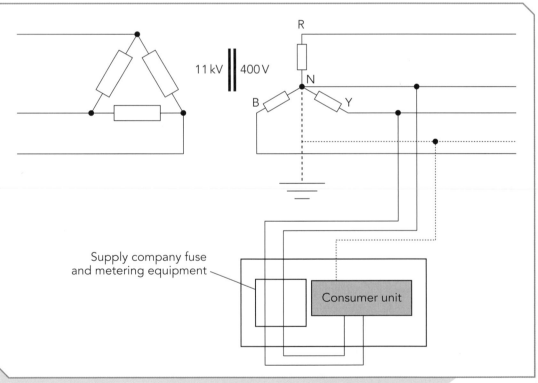

Figure 9.3: The arrival of a 230V TN–S supply into a domestic property.

Star and delta connections

As you can see from Figure 9.3, the windings in the transformers can be wired as a *star* or *delta*.

We tend to use the delta connection when we have a balanced load. This is because there is no need for a neutral connection and therefore only three wires are needed.

Consequently, we tend to find that this configuration is used for power transmission from power stations or to connect the windings of a three-phase motor.

In Figure 9.4 we have shown a three-phase load, which has been delta connected.

You can see that each leg of the load is connected across two of the lines. For example, R–Y, Y–B and B–R. We refer to the connection between phases as being the *line voltage*, which is shown on the drawing as VL.

Equally, if each line voltage is pushing current along, we refer to these currents as being *line currents*, which are represented on the drawing as IR, IY or IB.

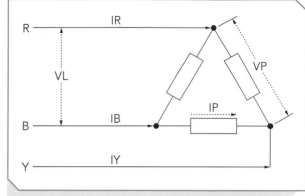

Figure 9.4: Delta connected three phase load.

These line currents are calculated as being the phasor sum of two *phase currents*, which are shown on the drawing as IP and represent the current in each leg of the load.

Similarly, the voltage across each leg of the load is referred to as the phase voltage (VP).

In a delta-connected balanced three-phase load, we are then able to state the following formulae:

$$VL = VP$$
$$L = \sqrt{3} \times P$$

Although we will prove this with an example later, you should note that a load connected in delta would draw three times the line current, and consequently three times as much power as the same load connected in star.

For this reason, induction motors are sometimes connected in star–delta. This means they start off in a star connection (with a reduced starting current) and are then switched to delta. In doing so, we reduce the heat that would otherwise be generated in the windings.

Star connection

Although we can have a balanced load connected in star (three-wire), we tend to use the star connection when we have an unbalanced load, i.e. one where the current in each of the phases is different. In this circumstance, one end of each of the three star-connected loops is connected to a central point; it is from this point that we take our neutral connection, which in turn is normally connected to earth. This is the three-phase four-wire system.

Another advantage of the star-connected system is that it allows us to have two voltages. One when we connect between any two phases (400 V) and another when we connect between any phase and neutral (230 V). You should note that we will also therefore have 230 V between any phase and earth.

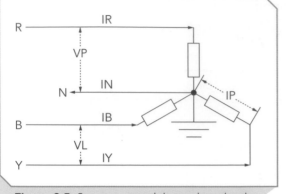

Figure 9.5: Star connected three-phase load.

In this diagram, we have shown a three-phase load that has been star connected.

As with delta, we refer to the connection made between phases as the *line voltage* and have shown this on the diagram as VL.

However, unlike delta, the *phase voltage* exists between any phase conductor and the neutral conductor. We have shown this on the diagram as VP.

Our *line currents* have been represented on the diagram by IR, IY and IB, with the *phase currents* being represented by IP.

In a star-connected load, the line currents and phase currents are the same, but the line voltage (400V) is greater than the phase voltage (230V).

In a star-connected load, we are therefore able to state the following formulae:

$$IL = IP$$

$$VL = \sqrt{3} \times VP$$

Using the star-connected load we have access to a 230V supply, which we use in most domestic and low-load situations.

Example

A three-phase star-connected supply feeds a delta-connected load as shown.

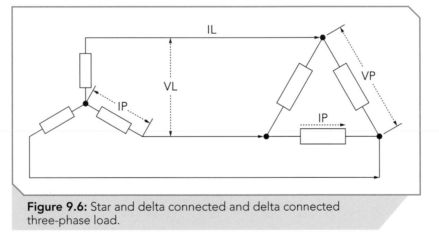

Figure 9.6: Star and delta connected and delta connected three-phase load.

If the star-connected phase voltage is 230V and the phase current is 20A, calculate:

➤ the line voltages and line currents in the star connection.

➤ the line and phase voltages and currents in the delta connection.

The star connection

In a star system the line current (IL) is equal to the phase current (IP). If we have been given IP as 20A, then IL must also be **20A**.

We find line voltage in a star connection using the formula VL = $\sqrt{3}$ × VP. $\sqrt{3}$, the square root of 3, is a constant with the value 1.732.

Therefore, if we substitute our values, we get: VL = 1.732 × 230 = **398V.**

Delta connection

In a delta system, the line current (IL) is 1.732 times greater than the phase current (IP).

We calculate this using the formula: $\mathbf{L} = \sqrt{3} \times P$

However, we know that IL is 20A, so if we transpose our formula and substitute our values, we get:

$$IP = \frac{L}{\sqrt{3}} = \frac{20}{1.732} = \mathbf{11.5A}$$

We know that for a delta connection, line voltage and phase voltage have the same values.

Therefore, VL = VP = **398V**.

Neutral currents

Where we have a balanced load, you have a three-phase system with three wires. However, it is more likely that we will find an unbalanced system and will therefore need to use a three-phase four-wire system. In such a system, we are saying that each line (R, Y, B) will have an unequal load and therefore the current in each line can be different. It becomes the job of the neutral conductor to carry this out-of-balance current.

ACTIVITY

Three identical loads of 30Ω resistance and 40Ω inductive reactance are connected to a 400V three-phase supply. Calculate the phase and line currents if the loads were connected:

1. in star.

2. in delta.

Three-phase transformers

The transformer is a widely used piece of electrical equipment and can be found in situations such as electricity distribution and electronic equipment. Its purpose is to transform voltage, which can enter the transformer at one level (input) and leave at another (output). When the output voltage is higher than the input voltage we have a *step-up* transformer; when the output voltage is lower than the input, we have a *step-down* transformer.

Transformers are rated in volt-amperes (VA), or, in the case of large power outputs, thousands of volts and amperes: *kVA rating*. The rating is always based on the *secondary winding*.

Where a transformer has a VA rating, this is the product of the secondary voltage and the secondary current.

The arrangement of the windings (three primary and three secondary) can then follow one of the following four patterns, where the windings are given as primary then secondary:

➤ star–star

➤ delta–delta

➤ star–delta

➤ delta–star

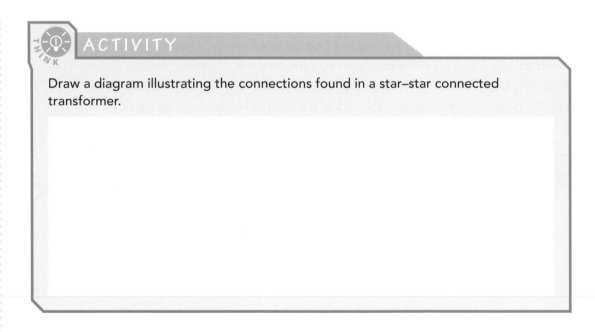

ACTIVITY

Draw a diagram illustrating the connections found in a star–star connected transformer.

Example calculation 1

A transformer having a 2 : 7 turns ratio is connected to a 230 V supply. Calculate the output voltage.

When we give transformer ratios, we give them in the order primary then secondary. Therefore, in this example we are saying that for every two windings on the primary winding, there are seven on the secondary.

Look at the formula:

$$\frac{V_p}{V_s} = \frac{N_p}{N_s}$$

We can transpose this to give:

$$V_s = V_p \times \frac{N_s}{N_p}$$

We don't know the exact number of turns involved, but do we need to if we know the ratio?

The ratio is 2:7, meaning that for every two turns on the primary, there will be seven turns on the secondary. If we had six turns on the primary, this would give us 21 turns on the secondary, but the ratio hasn't changed. We're still getting seven turns on the secondary for every two on the primary.

This means we insert the ratio into our formula:

$$V_s = \frac{V_p \times N_s}{N_p} = \frac{230 \times 7}{2} = \textbf{805 V}$$

To prove our earlier point about ratios, lets say that we know the number of turns in the windings to be 6 in the primary and 21 in the secondary. If we apply this to our formula we get:

$$V_s = \frac{V_p \times N_s}{N_p} = \frac{230 \times 21}{6} = \textbf{805 V}$$

ACTIVITY

1. A single-phase transformer, with 2,000 primary turns and 400 secondary turns, is fed from a 230 V ac supply. Find:
   - the secondary voltage

   - the volts per turn

2. A single-phase transformer is being used to supply a heating system. The transformer is fed from a 230 V 50 Hz ac supply and needs to provide an output voltage of 25 V. If the secondary current is 150 A and the secondary winding has 50 turns, find:
   - the output kVA of the transformer

   - the number of primary turns

   - the primary current

   - the volts per turn

Electrical properties

Inductance, reactance and capacitance

Inductance

The opposition of a coil to an alternating current due to its inductance and is called inductive reactance. Inductive reactance does not produce heat. It is measured in ohms. An ohm of inductive reactance – symbolised as XL – is the opposition equivalent to an ohm of resistance.

The ohmic value of the inductive reactance of a coil can be found from the expression:

$$XL = 2\pi fl$$

where XL stands for the inductive reactance in ohms, f for the frequency in hertz, and l for the inductance of the coil in Henries.

Capacitance

The capacity of an electrical capacitor may be defined as the quantity of charge it holds at unit electrical pressure. The term associated with this is *capacitance*.

The formula relating capacitive reactance, capacity and frequency is:

$$Xc = \frac{1}{2\pi fc}$$

where Xc stands for capacitive reactance in ohms, f for frequency in hertz and c for the capacitance in farads.

 ACTIVITY

1. A coil of 0.15H is connected in series with a 50 Ω resistor across a 100 V 50 Hz supply. Calculate:

   - the inductive reactance of the coil

   - the impedance of the circuit

   - the circuit current

2. A coil of 0.159H is connected in series with a 100Ω resistor across a 230V 50Hz supply. Calculate:

- the inductive reactance of the coil

- the circuit impedance

- the circuit current

Power factor

Power in an AC circuit

If we were to try and push something against a resistance, we would get hot and dissipate heat as we use up energy in completing the task. When current flows through a resistor, a similar thing happens, and power is used up in the form of energy pushing against this resistance.

Therefore, if a resistor (R) has a current (I) flowing through it for a certain time (t), then the power (energy being used per second) given in Watts, can be calculated by the formula:

$$P = I^2 \times R$$

What we are effectively saying is that the average power in a resistive circuit (one which is non-reactive, i.e. doesn't possess inductance or capacitance), can be found by the product of the readings of an ammeter and a voltmeter.

We call this type of power the *active power*.

When we look at the capacitive circuit, we find that current flows to the capacitor, but we have no power.

However, what we do have is voltage and current, but no average power. This means that our previous formula ($P = I^2 \times R$) is no longer useful. We therefore say that the result of voltage and current in this type of circuit is called *reactive power* and we express this in reactive volt-amperes (VAr).

Equally, we say that the current in a capacitive circuit, where there is no resistance and no dissipation of energy, is called *reactive current*.

In a circuit with resistance and reactance, there will be a phase angle between the voltage and current. This relationship is relevant, as power will only be expended in the resistive part of the circuit.

We also said that in a resistive circuit the voltage and current are in phase, and therefore this section of the current can be represented by the phasor Ip.

This part of the current is in the active section. We refer to this as the active current.

The actual (true) power of the circuit has to take on board the effect of the phase angle (cos θ). The ratio of these two statements is the power factor. Therefore:

$$\text{Power factor (cos } \theta) = \frac{\text{true power } (P)}{\text{apparent power } (S)} = \frac{V \times I \cos \theta}{V \times I} = \frac{\text{Watts}}{\text{Voltamperes}}$$

To summarise, what we perceive to be the power of a circuit (the apparent power) can also be the true power, as long as we have a unity power factor (1.0).

However, as long as we have a phase angle, then we have a difference between apparent power and reality (true power). This difference is the power factor (a value less than unity)

In reality, we will use a wattmeter to measure the true power and a voltmeter and ammeter to measure the apparent power.

Example 1

A resistor of 15 Ω has been connected in series with a capacitor of reactance 30 Ω.

If they are connected across a 230 V supply, establish both by calculation and by drawing a scaled power triangle, the following:

➤ the apparent power

➤ the true power

➤ the reactive power

➤ the power factor.

By calculation

In order to establish the elements of power, we must first find the current. To do this we need to find the impedance of the circuit:

$$Z = \sqrt{R^2 + X_c^2} = \sqrt{15^2 + 30^2} = \sqrt{225 + 900} = \sqrt{1,125}$$

therefore, $Z = 33.5 \, \Omega$

$$I = \frac{V}{Z} = \frac{230}{33.5} = 6.9 \, A$$

Apparent power

$V \times I = 230 \times 6.9 = 1587$ volt-amperes or **1.59 kVA**

Power factor

$$\frac{R}{Z} = \frac{15}{33.5} = 0.448 \text{ (leading)}$$

True power

True power can also be calculated by using the formula $I^2 \times R$.

Reactive power

Using Pythagoras' theorem and the formula $(VA)^2 = (W)^2 + (VAr)^2$, we transpose to give us:

$$\text{Reactive Power VAr} = \sqrt{(VA)^2 - (W)^2} = \sqrt{1{,}587^2 - 711^2}$$

Therefore, reactive power = 1,418.82 reactive volt-amperes or **1.42 kVAr**

Three-phase power

As we have seen in the previous section, we can find the power in a single-phase ac circuit by using the formula:

$$\text{Power} = V \times I \times \cos \theta$$

We could perhaps assume logically, that if this is the formula for one phase, then for three phases we should have three times as much, so multiply this formula by three.

That's not far from the truth, but if we follow that logic through, we must remember that this could only apply where we have a balanced three-phase load, i.e. one where we have the same current in each line. Or

$$\text{Power} = 3 \times V_{ph} \times I_{ph} \times \cos \theta$$

So, we can therefore say that for any three-phase balanced load, the formula to establish power is:

$$\text{Power} = \sqrt{3} \times (V_L \times I_L \times \cos \theta)$$

However, in the case of an unbalanced load, we need to calculate the power for each separate section and then add them together to get the total power.

Example 2

A balanced load of 10 Ω per phase is star-connected and supplied with 400 V 50 Hz at unity power factor. Calculate the:

➤ phase voltage

➤ line current

➤ total power consumed.

Phase voltage

$$V_L = \sqrt{3} \times V_P$$

Therefore, by transposition,

$$V_P = \frac{V_P}{\sqrt{3}} = \frac{400}{1.732} = 231 \text{ V}$$

Line current

$$I_L = I_P$$

therefore,

$$I_P = \frac{V_P}{R_P} = \frac{231}{10} = 23.1 \text{ A}$$

Total power

In a balanced system, power $= \sqrt{3} \times V_L \times I_L \times \cos \theta = 1.732 \times 400 \times 23.1 \times 1 = \mathbf{16\,k}$

1. Three coils of resistance 40 Ω and inductive reactance 30 Ω are connected in delta to a 400 V 50 Hz three-phase supply. Calculate:
   - the current in each coil

   - line current

   - total power

2. A small industrial estate is fed by a 400 V, three-phase, four-wire TN–S system. On the estate there are three factories connected to the system as follows:
   - factory A takes 50 kW at unity power factor
   - factory B takes 80 kVA at 0.6 lagging power factor
   - factory C takes 40 kVA at 0.7 leading power factor.

   Calculate the overall kW, kVA, kVAr and power factor for the system.

DC machines and AC motors

The main features of a DC machine are:

➤ the magnetic field system

➤ conductors mounted on the armature

➤ the commutator and brush-gear

➤ the rotation of the armature.

Any conductor carrying an electrical current also has a magnetic field associated with it. The strength of this field is dependent on the level of current flowing in the conductor. The direction of the magnetic field can be found by the use of the *right-hand rule*.

> The right-hand rule states that if you imagine you are grasping the *conductor in your right hand*, with your *thumb* pointing in the *direction in which the current is flowing*, then your *fingers* point in the *direction of the field around the conductor*.

If a current-carrying conductor is placed within a magnetic field, its own magnetic field will distort this field to cause a force, acting on the conductor, tending to move the conductor out of the field. The basic rule is that the current-carrying conductor tends to move at *right angles* to the magnetic field.

ACTIVITY

Draw a labelled diagram of Fleming's left-hand motor rule.

ACTIVITY

Draw simple line diagrams showing the circuit connections of the following DC motors.

DC series motor

DC shunt motor

DC compound motor

ACTIVITY

Complete the table using diagrams where appropriate to illustrate your answers.

Type of motor	Describe the operating principles of how this motor works. Use diagrams as necessary to help your explanation	State the use of this type of motor and explain its limitations
Single-phase AC motor, capacitor start		
Single-phase AC motor, induction start		
Single phase AC motor, universal motor		
Three-phase AC motor, squirrel cage		
Three-phase AC motor, wound rotor		
Inverter motor variable frequency drive		
Synchronous motor		

Starting and controlling motors

The direct-on-line starter

This is the simplest and cheapest method of starting squirrel-cage (induction) motors. The expression 'direct-on-line starting' means that the full supply voltage is directly connected to the stator of the motor by means of a contactor-starter, as shown in Figure 9.7.

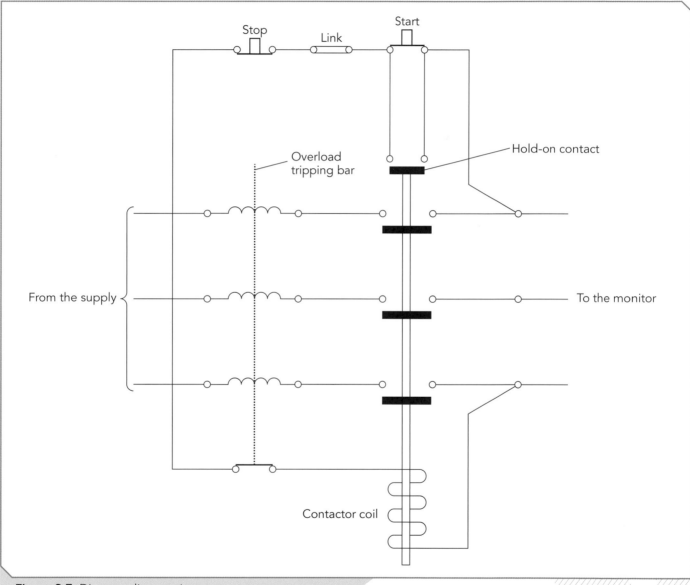

Figure 9.7: Direct-on-line starting.

Since the motor is at a standstill when the supply is first switched on, the initial starting current is heavy. This 'inrush' of current can be as high as 6–10 times the full load current. For example, a motor rated at 10A could have a starting current inrush as high as 60A, and the initial starting torque can be about 150 per cent of the full load torque. Thus, you may observe that motors 'jump' on starting if their mountings are not secure. As a result, direct-on-line starting is usually restricted to comparatively small motors with outputs of up to about 5kW.

Other methods of starting motors

As mentioned above, when switching on an induction motor with a direct-on-line starter, it can draw initial starting currents that are between 6–10 times the full-load current of the motor. This is acceptable for small motors up to about 5 kW, but for motors over this size consideration should be given to the installation of a starter that will limit the current on starting. The simplest and most economical way of achieving a lower starting current is by use of the hand-operated air-break star–delta starter.

ACTIVITY

Draw a diagram of the named starting methods and list the advantages and disadvantages for each method.

Star–delta

Rotor-resistance

Soft start

Electrical lighting systems

Illumination by means of electricity has been available for over 100 years. In that time it has changed in many ways, though many of the same ideas are still in use. The first type of electric lamp was the 'arc lamp', which used electrodes to draw an electron through the air. This was quite an unsophisticated use of electricity and many accidents and fires were caused by this use of electricity. Regulations had to be developed to control their use, and it is interesting that the first edition of the regulations was titled 'Rules and Regulations for the prevention of fire risks', introduced in 1882. The first lamp developed for indoor use was the carbon filament lamp. Although this was a dim lamp by modern standards, it was cleaner and far less dangerous than the exposed 'arc lamp'. There are now calculations involved in determining the correct amount of illumination required for these lamps.

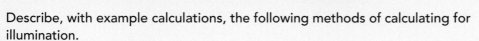

ACTIVITY

Describe, with example calculations, the following methods of calculating for illumination.

The inverse square law

The cosine law

The Lumen method

ACTIVITY

Lights (luminaires) are available in a variety of different types. Complete the table using diagrams where appropriate to illustrate your answers.

Type of luminaire	Operating principal (with diagram)	Limitations of this type of luminaire	How and where it is used
General lighting service (GLS) tungsten			
General lighting service (GLS) halogen			
Mercury vapour – low pressure			
Mercury vapour – high pressure			
Mercury vapour – metal halide			
Sodium vapour – low pressure			
Sodium vapour – high pressure			
Energy-saving, such as compact fluorescent lamps			
Light-emitting diode (LED)			

Electrical heating

ACTIVITY

There are two main methods of heating water electrically; either heating a large quantity stored in a tank or heating only what is required when it is needed.

With all types of heater it is important to ensure that the exposed and extraneous conductive parts are adequately bonded to earth. Water and electricity do not mix.

It is also important to ensure that the cables selected are of the correct size for full-load current, since no diversity is allowed for water heaters.

Label the diagrams below and describe the principle of operation of the various units.

Dual-element water heater

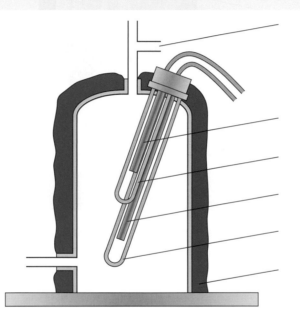

Cistern-type water heater

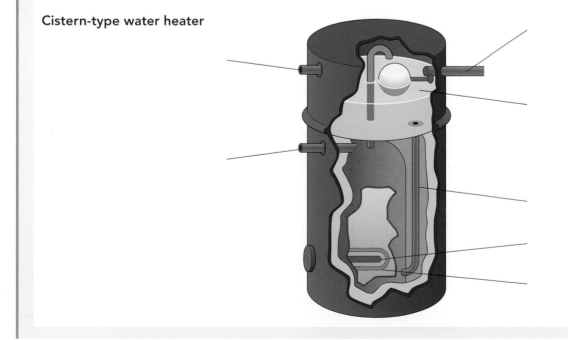

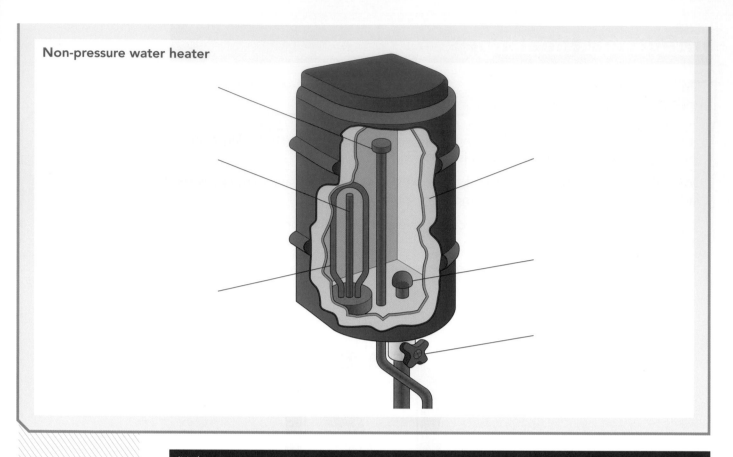

Non-pressure water heater

Electronics

In today's world, electricians need to learn about electronics because the use of circuits in things such as security alarms, telephones, dimmers, boiler controls and speed controllers have now brought electronics into general electrical installation work.

The following areas will be covered: resistors, capacitors, rectifiers, diodes, thermisters, diacs, triacs, transistors, thyristors, and invertors.

Resistors

There are two basic types of resistor: fixed and variable. The resistance value of a fixed resistor cannot be changed by mechanical means (though its normal value can be affected by temperature or other effects). Variable resistors have some means of adjustment (usually a spindle or slider). The method of construction, specifications and features of both fixed and variable resistor types vary, depending on what they are to be used for.

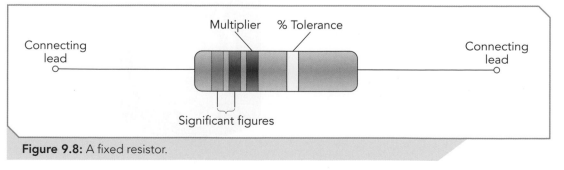

Figure 9.8: A fixed resistor.

ACTIVITY

Resistors are rated by the colour-coding chart, which includes reference to the band colour, number, multiplier and percentage tolerance.

Complete the table, filling in the values for multiplier band and tolerance.

Band colour	Number	Multiplier	Percentage tolerance
Black	0		
Brown	1		
Red	2		
Orange	3		
Yellow	4		
Green	5		
Blue	6		
Violet	7		
Grey	8		
White	9		
Gold (last band)			
Silver (last band)			
No colour (last band)			

ACTIVITY

Determine the value of the resistors colour-coded as follows:

1. Red, yellow, orange, gold

2. Red, orange, blue, gold

3. Brown, orange, yellow, silver

4. Black, brown, green, no colour

5. Red, green, orange, gold

Capacitors

Just as resistors enable us to introduce known amounts of resistance into a circuit to serve our purposes, so we can use components known as capacitors where needed in a circuit. Like resistance, capacitance always exists in circuits.

There are two major types of capacitor, fixed and variable, both of which are used in a wide range of electronic devices. Fixed capacitors can be further subdivided into electrolytic and non-electrolytic types. Together they represent the majority of the market.

All capacitors possess some resistance and inductance because of the nature of their construction. These undesirable properties result in limitations, which often determine their applications.

ACTIVITY

Draw a diagram of a fixed capacitor and a variable capacitor.

Fixed capacitor

Variable capacitor

ACTIVITY

The following electronic components are often found in electrical applications. Complete the table for these electronic components.

Electronic component	Operating principles – how it works	Application – where you would find this component
Fixed resistor		
Variable resistor		
Fixed capacitor		
Variable resistor		
Rectifiers		
Diodes		
Thermisters		
Diacs		
Triacs		
Transistors		
Thyristors		
Invertors		

Your questions answered...

I have often heard that current does not flow positive to negative but the other way around. Can you please explain this to me?

We know that a force (known as an electromotive force (emf)) is needed to cause this flow of electrons.

This has the quantity symbol E and the unit symbol V (volt). Any apparatus that produces an emf (such as a battery) is called a power source and will require wires or cables to be attached to its terminals to form a basic circuit.

If we take two dissimilar metal plates and place them in a chemical solution (known as an electrolyte), a reaction will take place in which electrons from one plate travel through the electrolyte and collect on the other plate. One plate now has an excess of electrons, which will make it more negative than positive.

Of course, the other plate will now have an excess of protons, which makes it more positive than negative. This is how a simple battery or cell works.

A wire, which has free outer electrons, can be used as a conductor by connecting it to the ends of the plates, as shown below.

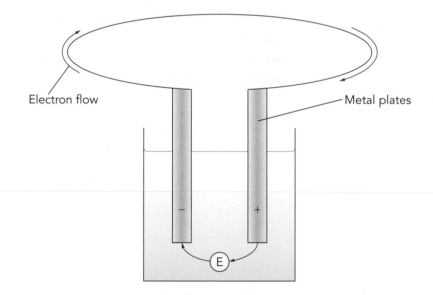

Because opposite charges are attracted towards each other, while like charges repel each other, you can see that the negative electrons will move from the negative plate, through the conductor towards the positive plate.

In other words, the flow is actually negative to positive through the conductor, not vice versa.

This drift of free electrons is what we know as electricity. This process will continue until the chemical action of the battery is exhausted and there is no longer a difference between the plates.

QUICK QUIZ

1. Name the four bands found in the colour code system for resistors and capacitors.

2. Choose a rhyme for remembering the colours in the resistor colour code system.

3. List and describe the different types of dielectric found in capacitors and name the three factors that the value of capacitance depends on.

4. Capacitors of 10 μF, 12 μF and 40 μF are connected in series and then in parallel. Calculate the effective capacitance for each connection.

5. Describe the depletion layer and explain how the depletion is achieved.

6. Describe the characteristic of zener diodes and list some of their applications.

7. Describe, with the aid of diagrams, the process for testing diodes.

8. Define the terms *mass* and *weight* and explain how they differ.

9. The power output of a motor is 250 W and the input is 1.5 A at 230 V. Calculate the percentage efficiency of the motor.

10. Calculate the current taken by a motor whose output power is 2.5 kW and efficiency is 78 per cent, when it is working from a 230 V supply.

Glossary

Accident report
A written account of an accident including near misses which need to meet the requirements of the employer and Health and Safety legislation.

Air pollutants
Chemicals, particulate matter or biological materials released into the atmosphere that cause harm or discomfort to humans or other living organisms, or which damage the natural environment.

Conductor
A material that conducts electricity.

Connection
A joint in non-flexible cables, which should be soldered, brazed, welded or made using mechanical clamps or with a compression joint.

Consumer unit
Is a box of fuses or circuit breakers, usually arranged in a single row.

Diagnosis
The analysis of problems within a faulty wiring system and the associated investigation.

Earthing
The process of connecting together all metalwork to prevent dangerous potential differences between different metals or between metals and earth. Correct earthing procedures prevent danger to life and risk of fire from excessive currents.

Efficiency
The efficiency of a system is the ratio of the output to the input.

Electron
A stable subatomic particle with a negative charge.

Emf
The electromotive force or the force that causes the flow of electrons.

Greenhouse gases
Gases in the atmosphere that trap the sun's energy and thereby contribute to rising surface temperatures. The main greenhouse gas that contributes to climate change is carbon dioxide (CO_2), a byproduct of burning fossil fuels.

Hazard
A situation that may be dangerous and has the potential to cause harm.

Insulator
A material that doesn't readily conduct electricity.

Molecule
A group of atoms bonded together.

Nucleus
The positively charged central core of an atom made up of protons – has a positive charge.

Personal protective equipment (PPE)
Protective clothing, head protection, goggles, gloves or other garments designed to protect the body from injury.

Proton
A stable subatomic particle occurring in all atoms – has a positive charge.

Pythagoras' theorem
Formula for calculating the length of sides in right-angled triangles. Named after Pythagoras, an ancient Greek mathematician.

Recycling
Passing a substance through a system that enables that substance to be reused. Waste recycling involves the collection of waste materials and the separation and clean up of those materials. Recycling waste means that fewer new products and consumables need to be produced, saving raw materials and reducing energy consumption.

Risk
The possibility that something dangerous may happen.

Risk assessment
A procedure that identifies potential risk of harm to people on the site. It is a legal requirement.

Shock protection
Protection against direct and indirect contact to prevent humans or livestock suffering from electric shock. Provided by barriers, covers, insulation, fuses, MCBs, RCDs and effective earthing.

Star point

Is the central point of joining three-wire star-connected loads. The neutral connection is normally taken from the star point which in turn, is normally connected to earth.

Sustainable development

Building developments needed to satisfy today's society should not compromise the potential for future generations to satisfy theirs. Consideration must be given to the long-term impact on the natural environment.

Testing

Undertaking a series of steps to check that an electrical installation is working safely, correctly and efficiently.

Zero carbon

A standard in energy production and use that treats homes as individual energy 'islands' which must generate all the power and heat they need. Current recommendations are that the 'built performance' emissions from new homes should not exceed:

➤ 10 kg CO_2(eq)/m²/year for detached houses.

➤ 11 kg CO_2(eq)/m²/year for other houses.

➤ 14 kg CO_2(eq)/m²/year for low rise apartment blocks.